D1395985

EXPLORING THE CHRISTIAN FAITH

By the same author:

THE REALLY PRACTICAL GUIDE TO PRIMARY R.E.
(Stanley Thornes, 1990)

Exploring the Christian Faith

*Notes for study groups
with points for discussion*

HUBERT J. SMITH

The Canterbury Press
Norwich

© Hubert J. Smith 1994

First published 1994 by The Canterbury Press Norwich
(a publishing imprint of Hymns Ancient & Modern Limited,
a registered charity)
St Mary's Works, St Mary's Plain,
Norwich, Norfolk, NR3 3BH

*All rights reserved. No part of this publication which is copyright may
be reproduced, stored in a retrieval sysem, or transmitted, in any form
or by any means, electronic, mechanical, photocopying, recording, or
otherwise, without the prior permission of the publisher.*

Hubert J. Smith has asserted his right under the Copyright, Designs
and Patents Act, 1988, to be identified as Author of this Work

British Library Cataloguing in Publication Data

A catalogue record for this book is available
from the British Library

ISBN 1-85311-080-9

*Typeset by Datix International Limited
Bungay, Suffolk and
Printed and bound in Great Britain by
St Edmundsbury Press Limited
Bury St Edmunds, Suffolk*

HOW TO USE THESE NOTES

These notes have been written for use in church study and discussion groups, of any Christian denomination. They are therefore not narrowly sectarian, and could prove to be useful in ecumenical groups where the members come from a variety of churches – or even from no church at all.

The aim is to encourage exploration and debate about issues which go right to the heart of Christian belief and practice. Because of this, some of the questions raised are very controversial: but controversy can be creative in itself, and it is often out of such argument that new ideas emerge. A discussion group in which all the members hold exactly the same views is likely to be at best very dull and at worst totally arid.

The brief introduction to each topic is not meant to be viewed as a thorough-going study. It should be treated as a pointer towards further enquiry, and it is highly probable that the discussion questions which follow the introduction will prove to be the most productive elements in the notes.

It is recommended that groups should not be too large. If the membership reaches ten, it is advisable to divide into smaller numbers. The group leader should try to ensure that everyone participates, and should not try to act as the resident expert whose opinion is final.

Each member of the group should have a copy of this book so that they can read the notes, preferably before the meeting. Copies of the Bible (in any version) should also be made available for reference.

TOPICS

<table>
<tr><td>

1

</td><td>

Belief in God

</td></tr>
</table>

● *This opening topic is fundamental to all that comes afterwards, so it will not be surprising to find that it is more substantial in its content than the rest. In order to break it up into manageable parts for study purposes, it has been divided into two sections, each with its own discussion points. The first section introduces some of the different ideas of God's nature which are to be found in the Bible, and raises the question of what God is believed to be like. The second section then moves to an exploration of a more philosophical kind: how do we know that God exists at all? Are there any proofs of his existence? Study groups are advised to deal with these two sections separately, because although they are clearly related, nevertheless they are quite different in their approaches, and in any case there is far too much material here to be covered in a single session.*

(a) WHAT IS GOD LIKE?

Christians believe in God. But are all Christians agreed about what God is like? The Apostles' Creed (which, incidentally, was not actually written by the Apostles) opens with the words 'I believe in God . . .' and goes on to describe him as 'the Father Almighty, maker of heaven and earth'. But this is not really much help. The creed was almost certainly meant as a personal statement of faith, for use by people who were about to be initiated into the Church through baptism, and was never intended to be used as a thorough-going analysis of developed theology. It shows only that this is the point at which Christian faith begins. We must take the matter further.

It is sometimes supposed that the Bible provides us with a detailed and coherent picture of God's nature, but closer examination shows that this is not the case. Careful study of the Old and New Testaments reveals that there are many different concepts of God to be found there, and they are not always entirely consistent with one another. Evidently the people of Bible times had a wide variety of ideas about what God is like. We can begin by looking at some of the ways in which God is portrayed in the Bible.

Old Testament pictures of God

In some parts of the Old Testament – especially the oldest parts – God is thought of as one deity among others. People imagined that every nation had its own god, who protected them in an exclusive kind of way. The ancient Israelites commonly believed that their own god (known to them by the name of YAHWEH) was more powerful than the others, but nevertheless he was not the only deity. We can see this idea brought out very plainly in the following passage:

Judges 2:11–15

● *Here it is said that the Israelites forsook their own god and worshipped the gods of other nations – identified in this instance as the Canaanite Baalim and Ashtaroth. Nowhere in this passage do we find it suggested that these other gods were false, or that they did not exist: they are represented as real rivals to the god of the Israelites.*

This belief in local tribal gods is sometimes known as Henotheism – a word which was coined in the middle of the nineteenth century to distinguish it from Monotheism (belief that there is only one God) and Polytheism (belief that there are many deities who are all equal in power and status). Most Biblical scholars consider that the religion of Israel was Henotheistic at first, and only gradually developed into Monotheism.

We can see a similar idea of God expressed in one of the Psalms. Look at:

2

Psalm 137:1–6

● *This psalm was written during the period when the Hebrew people were prisoners-of-war in the empire of Babylon (sixth century BC). The author evidently believed that God could be worshipped only in the Jerusalem Temple, and that it was impossible to worship on foreign territory. Here again is a very localised idea of God, though it is not entirely clear whether the writer of this psalm believed that God himself was absent from Babylon, or whether God would not accept worship from anywhere other than the Temple.*

Compare this with the sentiments of another psalm. Look at:

Psalm 139:1–12

● *This writer has a very different understanding of God. For him, it is impossible to go anywhere without finding that God is already there. Heaven and Hell, darkness and light are all the same to God, who dwells everywhere and knows everything. This omnipresent and omniscient God is very far removed from the territorial deity of Psalm 137.*

Gradually the people of the Old Testament came to an awareness that there is only one true God, and that idols simply do not have any reality. Look at:

Isaiah 45:18 to 46:7

● *This anonymous prophet of the sixth century BC (usually referred to as Deutero-Isaiah) categorically denies that other gods exist, and mocks those who manufacture their own deities. He points out that these home-made gods are incapable of doing anything at all.*

It was only when belief in one all-powerful and universal God came into currency that it was possible to think of him as having created the whole universe, and possessing dominion over it. Such a claim would have been impossible for those who thought only in terms of local gods with restricted authority, unless they were also dimly conscious of a 'higher' God than those with merely territorial concerns.

3

Now we turn to the Old Testament ideas about God's characteristics. Again, these are extremely varied. Where God is pictured as a tribal deity it is common to find him portrayed as a warrior, who leads his people into battle and guarantees victory over their enemies. We can see an example of this:

Exodus 15:3–5

- *In this passage it is openly said that God (YAHWEH) is a warrior, and that the escape from Egypt is to be counted as one of his greatest victories. There are many such passages to be found throughout the earlier parts of the Old Testament.*

Another dominant idea is that of God as a shepherd, who protects and guides his flock, ensuring that they have sufficient for their needs. The well-known Psalm 23 brings this out extremely well. Here, the warrior image has virtually disappeared, and in its place there is found a gentler conception of a devoted and loving deity. It was this image which dominated much of what Jesus had to say, both about God and about himself.

But by far the most telling imagery used about God is that of a parent – usually a father-figure, but not necessarily always in gender terminology. Indeed, in the book of Hosea (11:1–4) there is a very touching passage suggestive of maternal tenderness which contrasts very starkly with the warrior-like picture described above. God is thought of as having fatherlike characteristics: he gives life, he feeds his 'children', he teaches them, he controls and disciplines them, he protects them, and most of all he loves them. We have become so accustomed to the Biblical idea of God as a father-figure that it comes as something of a surprise to discover that in the religion of Islam this sort of imagery is considered highly improper. Muslims never refer to God as 'Father', on the ground that it suggests an over-intimate relationship with the holy deity.

4

New Testament pictures of God

In the New Testament the emphasis of all the writers is largely upon the way in which Jesus reveals God's nature and purposes to humankind. Jesus is the one who shows what God is like, and in that sense there is a much sharper focussing of thought. Supremely, Jesus shows a loving God who is prepared to sacrifice even himself because of his great love for his people. Sometimes the Old Testament ideas are recalled, as in the following passage:

Romans 1:19–25

● *In this passage St Paul gives the classical Old Testament picture of God as possessing everlasting power, and who cannot be represented by manufactured idols. Paul adds that God's nature can also be perceived within the created order (i.e. the universe) – another Old Testament idea, to be found for example in Psalm 19:1, except that here Paul gives it a moral content.*

The moral teachings of the New Testament also clearly echo the Old Testament ideas of a God who is himself just and fair, and who expects the same from his people. But it is the concept of God as 'Father' which tends to dominate, and in particular it is the relationship of Jesus to God which lies at the heart of New Testament thought. Jesus is God's obedient son, who lives in such close communion with his Father that he is 'one' with him. Thus, according to the author of the Fourth Gospel, whoever has seen Jesus has effectively seen God. As we have set aside a later topic about Jesus it is not necessary to develop this point here, except to lay stress upon the way in which the New Testament writers hold up Jesus as the revelation both of God and also of redeemed humanity.

DISCUSSION POINTS

1. Is there a right or wrong way of thinking about God's nature? If so, how do we know which is which?
2. How can Jesus the man reveal the nature of the eternal God?

5

3. If the writers of the Bible held differing views about what God is like, should we conclude that it is all a matter of personal opinion?

4. Can a Christian subscribe to the idea of a warrior-God?

5. If there is only one God, what are we to make of the other religions of the world?

6. If God is as powerful as the Bible claims, why does he allow so much to go wrong in his universe?

7. Is it true, as some have suggested, that the God described in the Old Testament is not the God revealed by Jesus Christ?

(b) DOES GOD EXIST?

The people who wrote the Bible took it for granted that God exists. Apart from one or two fleeting references (such as Psalm 14:1, repeated in Psalm 53:1), hardly anyone seems to have questioned the reality of God. His existence was axiomatic. But in modern times the issue is a serious one. Scientific discoveries have made people less ready to accept what cannot be proved, and today there are many who find it impossible to believe in the existence of God. Technically these people are known as ATHEISTS, and the word suggests that they have weighed the evidence and have concluded that there is no such being as God. They are to be distinguished from AGNOSTICS, who, strictly speaking, are those who admit that they do not know whether God exists or not. They are not persuaded one way or the other. In practice, however, atheists and agnostics are much the same because both are 'unbelievers'.

From time to time Christians are invited to state the grounds of their belief in God, and it is at this point that many find themselves in considerable difficulty. They sometimes respond with statements such as 'It's all a matter of faith', or perhaps 'I just believe, and that's that'. Such answers, though no doubt sincere, are hardly likely to be persuasive, and for this

6

reason Christian philosophers down the centuries have tried to demonstrate that there are genuine reasons why belief in God is sound. Of these philosophers, two in particular stand out as of great importance, namely, St Anselm of Canterbury and St Thomas Aquinas. Obviously there have been many others, but nearly all later arguments about God's existence are derived from these two thinkers, and we can look now at what they said.

St Anselm of Canterbury

Anselm was Archbishop of Canterbury in the eleventh century, and was actually a contemporary of William the Conqueror. He put forward what has since come to be known as the ONTOLOGICAL ARGUMENT – a somewhat grand name for a difficult piece of logical reasoning. Put in rather simplistic terms, it looks like this:

● *'God is the greatest being that it is possible to imagine.*
Therefore he must exist, because if he lacked existence it
would be possible to imagine a greater being who does exist.'

At first sight the argument seems silly – and it comes as no surprise to discover that even in his own time Anselm's argument was challenged. A monk by the name of Gaunilo retorted by saying that there is a big difference between claiming that God 'must' exist and saying that he actually does exist. Gaunilo pointed out that to imagine something to exist does not mean that it really is 'there'. He said that someone might imagine a very beautiful island in the middle of the ocean, and even imagine in great detail what it might look like: but this did not mean that such an island existed. To some people, Anselm's reasoning seems very much like that of those who say that because they believe in God, God must therefore be real – at least to them.

Anselm's argument, however, is not as childish as it may appear to be. It is really very subtle. He answered Gaunilo by

7

saying that the existence of God could not be compared to the existence of an imaginary island, and that Gaunilo had failed to understand the nature of the Ontological argument. There are many philosophers today who take Anselm's reasoning very seriously.

St Thomas Aquinas

Rather more persuasive arguments were put forward in the thirteenth century by St Thomas Aquinas, whose name is especially revered in the Roman Catholic Church. He disliked Anselm's way of reasoning, largely because it depended upon hypothesis, and he himself preferred to reason on the basis of actual experience and evidence. He proposed several arguments of a fairly detailed nature, but here we can note two in particular – expressed once again in a simplified way:

● *Everything that we see around us clearly has been caused by something before it. Every event was preceded by a prior event. Therefore there must have been a 'First Cause' for everything, and this we understand to be God.*

● *Everything that we see in the world is part of a highly complicated design, with things being dependent upon other things. Everything appears to have a place and a purpose within the overall pattern. Since such a world could not have come about by accident, it is therefore necessary to believe that it is the work of a Great Designer, and this we believe to be God.*

Although these arguments were put forward many centuries ago, they are still discussed today. However, they are not universally accepted as sound. First of all, it has been pointed out that if everything really does have a prior cause, then there cannot logically be a 'first cause' because it would immediately be an exception to the rule upon which the whole argument depends. It cuts the ground from under its own feet, because the 'first cause' would need to have a prior cause too.

8

Second, not everyone is convinced that there is a genuine pattern or design evident in the universe. Some consider that the alleged design is no more than our human way of looking at things, and that in reality the universe is a tangled mass of elements which are competing with each other rather than providing mutual support. And of course it therefore follows that if there is no genuine design, then we cannot conclude that there is a Great Designer.

Third, many philosophers have remarked that even if it could be shown that there is a First Cause or a Great Designer, it does not necessarily follow that, as St Thomas Aquinas claimed, 'this is what we believe to be God'. Certainly neither of the arguments leads to proof of the existence of the kind of God of whom the Bible speaks – that is, a God who has a special loving relationship with human beings. The so-called 'proofs' may indeed point in the general direction of some almighty power or force, but they do not (and cannot) lead to a fully-developed Christian belief in the God revealed in the person and work of Jesus Christ.

If all this seems somewhat negative, it is currently being argued that the concept of 'proof' is the product of a scientific way of thinking, and that since science, by its very nature, can deal only with the world of verifiable 'things' it cannot be summoned to give a verdict upon matters of religious faith. If it tries to do so, it steps outside its proper sphere and thereby ceases to be genuinely scientific. Therefore the person who believes in God need not be too anxious if his or her beliefs fail the tests of scientific or logical enquiry. There are other more appropriate tests, which may not succeed in convincing the sceptical but will certainly satisfy the believer.

DISCUSSION POINTS

1. **Are there any contemporary arguments which might persuade a non-Christian that God exists? Are the arguments of Anselm and Aquinas still acceptable?**

2. If it could be proved that God exists, would there still be any need for religious faith?

3. 'God is a theory proposed by people who don't understand the world around them. One day, science will make belief in God unnecessary.' Do you agree?

4. Are there any arguments against the existence of God? If so, what are they?

5. Is there any difference between a religious belief which is reached through reasoning and one which is reached through simple faith?

6. Do the arguments for the existence of God also point towards the existence of a Devil?

2	The person of Jesus

The central figure in the Christian faith

The central figure in Christianity is Jesus of Nazareth. Every one of the books in the New Testament makes reference to him, though not always in the same way. The letters of St Paul, for example, concentrate upon the outcome of Jesus' death and resurrection, while the four Gospels put their emphasis upon his life and work, leading up to his crucifixion and the discovery of the empty tomb. But all of them, in their own ways, make it clear that he is both the founder and the foundation-stone of Christian faith. But what does this mean?

What was special about Jesus?

It could mean that the most significant thing about Jesus was his teachings and his personal example, which his supporters tried to follow. Or it could mean that he became a martyr, and his memory was perpetuated for that reason. Both of these possibilities have at some time been proposed, but neither is an adequate description of the position which Jesus holds within the Christian faith.

The best way to establish Jesus' position in Christianity is to look at what the New Testament writers actually say about him. Look in particular at the following passages:

Mark 1:7–11

● *In this passage St Mark sets out the theme of his Gospel, which is his conviction that Jesus is 'the Son of God'. The whole of the book is dedicated to demonstrating that this is true, and virtually everything that Mark says about Jesus*

11

is directed towards revealing his divine nature. The various incidents in Jesus' life are not written down merely to keep a record of what happened: they are all chosen and presented as clues to his true identity. When Mark tells of what Jesus did, he wants his readers to respond with the question 'Who is this?' (see, for example, Mark 1:23–28, Mark 2:6–7, and Mark 4:35–41). Then, when they have been prompted to ask that question, he wants them to answer it for themselves and to recognise that Jesus is the Son of God.

John 20:31

● *Here the author of the Fourth Gospel explains his purpose in writing his account of Jesus' life. He, like Mark, wants to encourage belief that Jesus is the Christ, the Son of God, because that belief will effectively bring 'new life' to those who accept it. Like the other Gospel writers, he was not concerned to produce a biography of Jesus, but rather wanted to present a 'religious proposition' about Jesus' true nature.*

Look also at what St Paul said in his letter to the Romans (almost certainly written before the four Gospels, though in the New Testament collection it is placed after them):

Romans 1:1–6

● *Paul is explaining about the essence of his 'gospel' or good news. He says it is about God's Son (Jesus), who was an ordinary man in the physical sense, but also Son of God by virtue of his resurrection from the dead.*

Look in particular at two highly significant passages embodied in Paul's letters:

Philippians 2:5–11

● *This remarkable statement has been the subject of much discussion among Christian scholars, and it makes claims for Jesus which go far beyond the idea that he was just 'a good man'.*

Colossians 1:13–20 (also 3:9)

● *Once again, here are claims that Jesus was not only the Son of God, but that he actually participated in the act of creation, and that the 'complete being of God' is to be found within him.*

It is clear from these few examples alone that Christianity is not really about a way of life (though of course that comes into it), but is much more about believing in the authority of Jesus and the difference which his life, death and resurrection have brought about.

The birth narratives

Look at the two narratives of Jesus' birth (Matthew 1:18 to 2:23, and Luke 1:26 to 2:38). These are lengthy passages, but both of them contain numerous clues to what the two writers were trying to say. One of them (St Matthew) is concerned to show that Jesus was the expected Jewish Messiah who had come to fulfil God's promises to the Chosen People, and the other (St Luke) regards Jesus as having a wider significance, in that he is the Saviour of the world.

There is a good deal of debate going on within the Christian Church today about whether the birth of Jesus was 'miraculous' in the sense that the narratives propose, i.e., that he did not have a human father: but there is no argument that his birth was special in the sense that he somehow combined both humanity and divinity within his own person.

The humanity and divinity of Jesus

Christian theologians have always struggled with this doctrine of Jesus' 'double nature'. The theological science of CHRIST-OLOGY has developed as an approach to this. It seeks to clarify the apparent dilemma inherent in the claim that Jesus was both fully human and also fully divine, without compromising either of those two affirmations.

13

From time to time various simplistic 'solutions' have been put forward. One of the most outwardly attractive proposals became known as DOCETISM, which is a term derived from a Greek word meaning 'to seem to be' or 'to appear'. This theory proposed that Jesus only seemed to be human on the surface, and went through the motions of living a normal human life, but that in reality he was a 'spirit', incapable of being harmed or corrupted by the physical world. This idea probably emerged out of a wider philosophical outlook generally known as Gnosticism, but it certainly caused a lot of trouble for the early Christians who were trying to sort out their theology. Docetism still lingers on in various guises in modern times, and can be found in some of the sects and groups which are on the fringe of mainstream Christianity; but it has always been denounced by orthodox teachers as an inadequate way of 'explaining' the nature of Jesus.

Another solution was proposed by some who said that Jesus was a human being in the fullest sense during his life on earth, but that this was possible only because he had voluntarily laid aside his divine status. The implication of this, of course, is that he was not divine at all, except in the sense that he could have 'opted out' of his full humanity at any point in his earthly life.

One of the central questions raised in the early Church was that of whether Jesus had been born with a divine nature, or whether he was 'adopted' by God as a kind of seal of approval for his saintly life. Look at the following passage:

Mark 1:9–11

● *Some commentators have suggested that this represents an adoption ceremony, at which Jesus was given his special status as God's Son, and that this is why St Mark's Gospel does not contain an account of his special birth. Others argue that Mark did not really hold such a view, and that this passage should not be taken out of context.*

14

The standpoint of St Paul

Paul's position in this matter was clear. He approached it from several directions, but one of his most compelling analogies lay in his claim that Jesus' main work was that of 'reconciling' humanity with God, rather in the manner of 'bridge-building' (see II Corinthians 5:18–21). If we follow this useful analogy through a little further we see that if a bridge is to serve its purpose of linking two things together, then that bridge must of necessity be securely attached at both sides, or it cannot work. Thus Jesus had to be both fully divine and also fully human. Paul also adds that it is this 'reconciling' ministry which has been handed on to the Christian Church as its continuing duty.

The death of Jesus and the death of God?

At the heart of this question of Jesus' nature lies the issue of his death. How could it be said that God's Son 'died'? Once again, various theories have been proposed, including the idea that it was only Jesus the man who died, but Jesus the Son of God did not, and that it was this divine 'part' of Jesus which was resurrected, leaving his physical body behind. Needless to say, this idea has never been accepted into Christian orthodoxy because it leaves far too many loose ends – and groups are encouraged to think about what these loose ends might be.

DISCUSSION POINTS

1. Is the debate about Jesus' true nature merely an exercise for theologians, or is it crucial for Christian faith?

2. If Jesus was fully God as well as fully human, what does this imply as far as his suffering and death are concerned?

3. What do you understand by the Church's 'ministry of reconciliation'?

15

4. Can there be genuine Christian faith based on the belief
    that it is the teachings and the example of Jesus alone
    which are at the heart of the Christian religion?

3	The Holy Spirit

The Holy Spirit in the Old Testament

The Christian teaching about the Holy Spirit has its roots in the Old Testament, where it is said that God's Spirit was at work in several ways. Sometimes the Spirit is referred to as God's 'breath': the Hebrew word 'ruach' suggests the idea of God breathing his life into humankind (see Genesis 2:7), and this image very powerfully conveys the idea that 'Spirit' and 'Life' go hand in hand.

It is also said that God's Spirit 'inspired' particular people to do remarkable things. Look at the following passages in the Old Testament:

Exodus 35:30 to 36:1

● *In this passage it is said that a man named Bezalel was enabled by God's Spirit to become skilled in all sorts of crafts, and that (with another man, Aholiab) he was also inspired to teach those skills to others. Possibly this divine inspiration was connected with the fact that the craftsmanship was to be used in the religious context of the sanctuary.*

Isaiah 61:1–3

● *These verses come from an anonymous prophet generally referred to as Third Isaiah ('Trito-Isaiah'), whose teachings probably lay behind the closing chapters of this book. They reflect the belief that a true prophet is one who is empowered (i.e. by God's Spirit) to proclaim God's word.*

According to the Old Testament the Spirit of God is

17

responsible for bestowing other qualities, such as wisdom and intellectual gifts, and in particular the expected Messiah would be recognised by his possession of the Spirit (see Isaiah 11:2).

The Old Testament references to God's Spirit are frequently no more than a conventional device for avoiding the suggestion that God deals with people in a direct way. In early Hebrew thought it was sometimes considered improper to suggest that God 'spoke' face to face with people: this gave rise to the introduction of intermediaries such as angels (see the story of the Burning Bush in Exodus 3, where the writer or editor clearly had reservations about suggesting that God confronted Moses directly. In verse 2 it is said that it was an angel who appeared in the bush, but later it is openly suggested that it was God himself). The point being made here is that sometimes the Old Testament references to God's Spirit are no more than conventional ways of saying that God did particular things.

The Holy Spirit in the New Testament

The idea of the Holy Spirit (or the Spirit of God) is developed much further in the New Testament, especially in the Gospel of Luke, which has actually been described as 'the Gospel of the Holy Spirit'. According to Luke the Holy Spirit was responsible for the conception of Jesus (Luke 1:35), and was bestowed upon him in a special way at his baptism (see Luke 3:21–22). The involvement of the Spirit is also stressed in the story of the temptations of Jesus (see Luke 4:1–2), in the account of Jesus' work in Galilee (see Luke 4:14), and in the response of Jesus after the return of the seventy-two disciples who had been sent on a special mission (see Luke 10:21).

Luke's deep interest in the activity of God's Spirit is further reflected in the book of Acts, which forms the second volume of his work. Look at:

Acts 2:1–21

- *Here, Luke emphasises his belief that it was the same Holy Spirit which gave power to the followers of Jesus, thus placing them in a direct line of continuity with their master and providing them with the same source of strength. A little further in the same passage (see Acts 2:37–39) Peter tells those who were listening to the preaching that they were to present themselves for baptism, and they would also receive 'the gift of the Holy Spirit'.*

In the Fourth Gospel there is a somewhat different line of development. According to this writer the Holy Spirit has a special function, which appears to lie in the future, after Jesus has gone from the company of his disciples. Look at:

John 14:15–26 and John 15:26

- *Here the work of the Holy Spirit is described in terms of 'guidance'. It involves the task of revealing and expounding further truth, and of validating and bearing witness to Christ's work.*

The writings of St Paul show that he also gave a central place to the idea of the Holy Spirit, and sometimes he seems to place the Spirit and Christ so closely together that they become virtually indistinguishable. He speaks about 'life in the Spirit' in the same way as he speaks of 'life in Christ', and the work of the Spirit is merged with the work of the risen Christ. Look at:

I Corinthians 6:16–20

- *Paul is saying that the Christian should honour God not only with the mind but also with the body, and in this passage he brings together God, Christ, and the Holy Spirit as if they were all one. It is in passages of this nature that we find clues to the emerging doctrine of the Trinity.*

The Holy Spirit in the life of the Church

Although the Holy Spirit figures prominently in both the Old and the New Testaments, it took a long time for the Church to work out its theology and to clarify its doctrinal position. This was due in no small part to the confusion caused by various heretical groups such as the Montanists (who taught that the Holy Spirit would soon be given afresh to the Church, and laid down an extremely strict code of discipline) and the Pneumatomachi who absolutely denied the divinity of the Holy Spirit. It was only in the latter part of the fourth century that a clear doctrine of the Holy Spirit was formulated at the Council of Constantinople.

Throughout Christian history the Church has been aware of the need to keep the doctrine of the Holy Spirit under control. Unless some sort of check is kept upon it, there is an inherent danger that all kinds of beliefs and practices might be justified by the claim that they are evidence of the Spirit at work. This danger was recognised even in the New Testament period. Look at the following passage:

I John 4:1–3

- *Here the author of this short letter is conscious that false teachings can easily find their way into the Church through people who claim to be inspired by the Holy Spirit, and he suggests a way of putting those claims to the test.*

Down the centuries, the largest of all the Christian churches (the Roman Catholic Church) has sought to maintain spiritual stability by using its traditions as a kind of brake upon over-enthusiastic claims and practices. This is also true of the Anglican churches, though perhaps to a somewhat lesser degree. Other churches have put the doctrine of the Holy Spirit at the top of their agenda in matters of church life, and the best example here is that of the Pentecostals. In what is undoubtedly the most thorough-going and scholarly study of Pentecostalism, the following passage occurs:

'In what way have we departed from the commandments of
God, so that the gifts of the Holy Spirit, the healing of the
sick, prophecy, and speaking in tongues have disappeared, and
the church has become lifeless and powerless? How can we
overcome its "deepfreeze theology"? What must we do for the
wind of revival to begin to blow again, and the "showers of
blessing" to descend once more?' (Walter J. Hollenweger, *The
Pentecostals*, SCM Press 1972, p. 321).

Other denominations such as the Baptists and the United
Reformed Church have structured their organizations largely
on the principle of 'government by the Holy Spirit', claiming
that the regular meetings of their church members are
essentially occasions when the will of Christ for his people is
revealed through prayerful thought. It is sometimes wrongly
imagined that these churches are democratic in their outlook,
but in reality they regard themselves as being faithful to the
Biblical instruction to 'hear what the Spirit is saying to the
churches' (see Revelation 2:29).

DISCUSSION POINTS

1. What answer would you give to the question posed in the
    book on the Pentecostals, quoted above?

2. Suggest ways in which claims of 'inspiration' can be put
    to the test.

3. Is the doctrine of the Holy Spirit a loophole through
    which cranks and eccentrics can influence the churches?

4. Can you detect any consistent understanding of the
    nature of the Holy Spirit in the New Testament, or does
    each writer have his own views?

5. If a group of Christians meets prayerfully together, is
    there any guarantee that they are more likely to be led
    by the Holy Spirit than a Christian praying on his/her
    own?

4 | The Doctrine of the Trinity

Although Christianity professes belief in one God (Monotheism), yet it has developed a doctrine which has given rise to charges of preaching that there are actually three – God the Father, God the Son, and God the Holy Spirit. This doctrine of the Trinity has frequently been misunderstood and misinterpreted. For example, in the Qur'an (the sacred book of Islam) there is a passage which instructs Muslims not to accept a Trinitarian teaching:

- *'People of the Book, go not beyond the bounds in your religion, and say not as to God but the truth. The Messiah, Jesus son of Mary, was only the Messenger of God, and His Word that He committed to Mary, and a Spirit from Him. So believe in God and His Messengers, and say not, "Three". Refrain; better is it for you. God is only One God.' (Sura IV.166 in A. J. Arberry's translation, OUP 1964)*

There appears to be some confusion here, because the Trinity is apparently thought to consist of God, Jesus and Mary. But whatever is the correct understanding of this passage, it is obvious that the very notion of God being 'Three' is regarded as wrong, and Muslims are commanded not to accept it.

Throughout Christian history there have been those who have felt uncomfortable with the doctrine of a God who is said to be 'Three in One and One in Three'. During the second and third centuries there grew up a movement which was intended to protect the idea of the unity or one-ness of God. This became known as Monarchianism, and it asserted that although Jesus shared in the nature of God he was subordinate to him and therefore not God in the fullest sense.

In more recent times this kind of thinking was revived in the Unitarian Movement, which flourished in the nineteenth century under the leadership of scholars such as the Englishman James Martineau and the American Theodore Parker, though the Unitarians often claim that they owe their true beginnings to John Biddle in the seventeenth century.

The Trinity in the Old Testament

It is difficult to find any convincing passages in the Old Testament to support the idea that God has a three-fold nature, although there has been no lack of inventiveness in looking for them. Almost anything which contains the idea of 'three' has at some time been put forward as evidence of a Trinitarian principle. The most telling Old Testament contribution is found in the early parts where God is sometimes referred to in a plural form. The name ELOHIM (represented in the English translation as 'God', distinguishing it from 'the LORD', which represents the name YAHWEH) is actually a plural form. In the book of Genesis we find passages where the 'royal we' is used with reference to God (see Genesis 1:26 and Genesis 11:7). Some scholars regard these as evidence of a 'corporate' concept of God, though we must not rush ahead and make over-zealous claims that we have found references to the Trinity.

The Trinity in the New Testament

The actual word 'Trinity' does not appear anywhere in the Bible, but the idea of God having a threefold nature certainly does. The classical text here is found in St Matthew's Gospel, chapter 28 verse 19, where Jesus is reported as instructing his followers to baptise converts 'in the name of the Father, and of the Son, and of the Holy Spirit'. Many commentators have found difficulty in accepting that Jesus could have used this formula, but there is no evidence from early manuscripts that the words might have been added later.

The Fourth Gospel seems to support a Trinitarian outlook, in that it presents Jesus as identifying himself closely with both the Father and the Holy Spirit, and St Paul makes a further contribution in his correspondence with the church in Corinth. Look at the following passages:

John 14:11–21

● *Here Jesus says explicitly that he is 'in the Father' and that the Father is 'in him', and adds that the Father will send the Spirit who will remain with the disciples for ever. The bringing together of these three can be understood as a manifestation of the same God in three ways.*

I Corinthians 12:4–6

● *In this passage St Paul expounds the idea of one God expressing himself in a variety of ways.*

This kind of thinking, especially that of St Paul, derives from the traditional Hebrew concept of CORPORATE PERSONALITY. People were not thought of as separate individuals, totally independent of others: rather, they belonged to a community, and shared their characteristics and talents with one another. If one member of that community (especially the family group) committed an offence, then all were considered to be guilty, and conversely if one had cause for rejoicing, all shared that joy. St Paul uses this idea to elaborate upon what it means to be a member of the Christian community (see I Corinthians 12:1–26).

The theological need for a Trinitarian doctrine

The doctrine of the Trinity really grew out of the Church's need to work out its theology, and especially its understanding of the nature of God as revealed in the person of Christ and in the experience of the Holy Spirit. To talk in terms of three Gods would have been totally unacceptable, yet at the same time there was a need to match the doctrine to the Christian experience of God's continuing activity in the Church. It was this which produced the Trinitarian idea, and it has always been referred to as a 'mystery' because it is impossible to rationalise it. Although it uses the terminology of mathematics, it is not a mathematical concept, and any discussion of how three can be said to equal one is not a mathematical but a theological problem.

Perhaps the most straightforward way of 'explaining' the doctrine of the Trinity is to say that it embodies the Christian experience of God's three ways of being God. He is known in his fatherly nature, through creation: he is known in his nature as Son, through the person and work of Jesus Christ: and he is known in his spiritual nature, through the invisible but nevertheless real activity of the Holy Spirit in the life of the Church. These are three distinct perceptions, but they all point to the one God.

DISCUSSION POINTS

1. Does the doctrine of the Trinity serve any real purpose in Christian belief and life?

2. Is there a case for claiming that God reveals his nature in more than three ways, and if so, what are they?

3. It has been suggested that if a Christian lays more emphasis upon one Person of the Trinity than upon the others, an unbalanced understanding of God's full nature will result. Do you agree?

4. Does the idea that there is variety within the Godhead suggest that there is room for variety within the Church – that is to say, a kind of variety which does not imply division?

5 | A Christian view of Human Nature

The Christian religion is not only about God. It is also about the human race. We therefore cannot understand the faith unless we explore the nature of human beings, as perceived in Christian tradition. In other words, if we are to gain a proper awareness of Christianity we must examine its 'doctrine of man' (using the word 'man' in its broadest sense of 'humankind').

Look at the following passage:

Psalm 8:3–8

● *In this psalm the writer asks a fundamental question: what is the nature of humankind in relation to the almightiness of God? How can the God who made the universe possibly be interested in us?*

He then goes on to claim that mankind has pride of place in God's creation, having been made second only to God himself (the translation here is somewhat obscure, and group members should refer to as many versions of the text as they can find).

Mankind as God's crowning achievement

The notion that the human race is the crowning achievement of God's creation is explicitly stated in the two creation narratives in the book of Genesis. We can look at the later one first:

Genesis 1:1 to 2:4a

● *This is sometimes called the 'priestly' account of creation, because it bears the marks of the kind of liturgical poem used in the Jewish Temple. The supremacy of the human*

26

race is evidenced by the fact that according to the writer of his narrative God makes mankind 'to rule' over everything else.

Now look at the second creation narrative, which scholars believe to have originated at an earlier date:

Genesis 2:4b to 3:24

● *In this very ancient tradition, belief in the supremacy of the human race is expressed in the idea that after God had made the physical world, mankind was the first of all the living creatures. God's own breath is put into the man, and all the animals are then paraded before 'Adam' in order that they should be 'named' (i.e. given their place under Adam's authority).*

Mankind as 'fallen'

The Biblical view of human nature seems therefore to be quite clear. Man is made 'in the image of God', and is given authority to rule the world. However, things are not quite that straightforward. It is also said that human beings have defaced their godly image through disobedience against God's laws, and have lost their status. This is the classical Christian doctrine of the 'fall' of mankind. Because human beings have deliberately separated themselves from God they are now said to be in a condition of weakness, unable to help themselves.

We can see a very powerful description of humanity in its 'fallen' state (i.e. in its 'Godless' condition) in St Paul's letter to the Romans. Look in particular at:

Romans 1:18–32

● *This very severe picture suggests that mankind has no redeeming features whatsoever, but has 'fallen' to such depths that there is no hope of recovery except by the direct intervention of God. There is nothing in this description to suggest that there is 'some good in everyone'.*

The Biblical picture of humanity is thus seen to be somewhat contradictory, in the sense that both the dignity and also the corruption of mankind are highlighted. Mankind is a sort of riddle, aptly described by Shakespeare:

'What a piece of work is a man! How noble in reason! how infinite in faculty! in form, in moving, how express and admirable! in action how like an angel! in apprehension how like a god! the beauty of the world! the paragon of animals! And yet, to me, what is this quintessence of dust? man delights not me; no, nor woman neither'. (*Hamlet* II. ii. 316)

Alexander Pope (1688–1744) wrote in a similar fashion:

'Chaos of thought and passion, all confused; Still by himself abused, or disabused; Created half to rise, and half to fall; Great Lord of all things, yet a prey to all; Sole judge of truth, in endless error hurled: The glory, jest, and riddle of the world!'. (*An Essay on Man*, II. 13)

These quotations accurately reflect the Biblical analysis of mankind as a contradictory being who is potentially capable of much but constantly falls prey to his own cleverness.

Mankind as a corporate being

Alongside the idea of humanity as 'fallen' there runs in the Bible another important concept, which has to do with the relation of the individual to the wider community. Again there is a curious balance of opposites evident. On the one hand it is said that people are gregarious and communal beings, for whom it is unnatural to be alone. They share a common life, and have a mutual responsibility for one another. No one person is ever truly isolated – an idea taken up by the Christian poet John Donne (c. 1571–1631):

'No man is an Island, entire of itself; every man is a piece of the Continent, a part of the main'. (*Devotions*, XII)

But on the other hand we also find the recognition that there is such a thing as individual responsibility and individual guilt. People cannot lay the blame for their faults upon the fact that they 'caught' their weaknesses from others. This is brought out, for example, in the book of the prophet Ezekiel. Look at:

Ezekiel 18:1–4

- *Here the prophet insists that people must accept responsibility for their own actions. The popular belief that 'the sins of the fathers are visited upon the children' is countered by the affirmation that it is the actual soul which offends which must be punished.*

The New Testament view of humanity

These ideas follow through from the Old Testament into the New, but a fresh dimension is added through the contact which the Hebrew world had begun to make with the thinking of the Greeks, following the achievements of Alexander the Great. In Greek thought a human being was rather like a body with a soul inside it, and the two were commonly distinguished. At death it was believed that the body decayed, while the soul was set free to live in a new and unfettered way. But in Hebrew thought, a human being was a unique combination of the 'material' and the 'spiritual', expressed in the idea of God breathing his soul (or 'spirit') into human beings and thereby giving them life. The body and the soul are thus considered to be inseparable, neither being able to enjoy a proper existence without the other.

The combining of God's 'life' with humanity is what lies behind the Biblical teaching about the incarnation. Christ is looked upon as the beginning of a new creation, when mankind is made afresh. He is in a sense the new Adam – an idea made quite explicit by St Paul. Look at the following:

Romans 5:12–17

- *It is plain that in this passage Paul is making a direct link between the 'old man' (Adam) and the 'new man' (Jesus Christ).*

This is taken up in early Christian thought in the teaching that a Christian must be 'born again' (see John 3:1–8), that is to say, a new act of creation must take place if mankind's corrupt nature is to be replaced by a new quality of life.

The teaching of the New Testament about the incarnation of God in Jesus Christ gives a new and important dimension to the understanding of humanity. When the author of the Fourth Gospel says that 'the Word became Flesh' (See John 1:14) he is making a claim which would have astounded writers of the Old Testament. To suggest that God could or would actually enter human experience in that way would have seemed to be a denial of God's divine holiness, but in reality it is more in the nature of an 'ennobling of human nature'. It is seen as the ultimate act of a God who identifies so closely with his people that he shares their humanity with them.

It is this 'sanctification' of the human race which gives Christians their deepest reason for treating humanity seriously. It means that it is in the service of human beings that God himself is served.

DISCUSSION POINTS

1. In the light of what scientific discovery has revealed about the origins of the human race, is it still possible to claim that humanity is God's crowning achievement?

2. Does the story of the Fall of Mankind ring true to contemporary experience? Does it have to be taken literally to be of value?

3. Is St Paul too harsh in his description of humanity without God? Ought a Christian to see at least a spark of good in people?

4. How can we, as human beings, balance our need for company with our insistence upon being independent?

5. What do you think Jesus meant when he told Nicodemus about the necessity to be 'born again'?

6. If Jesus shared fully in human nature, does this mean that he shared in the 'fallen' condition of mankind? If not, how can he be said to be like us?

7. Is it true that the service of humanity is also the service of God?

6 The essence of the Christian Gospel

What is the Christian Gospel? Or, to put it another way, what is the central message of the Christian religion? Many would say that it is summed up in the words 'Love your neighbour', or even 'Do unto others as you would wish them to do to you'. But these are unsatisfactory as summaries of the Gospel, for several reasons:

(a) these are not unique to Christianity: other faiths teach these same principles:

(b) these are not really religious principles; they are moral or ethical precepts:

(c) Christianity actually teaches that these principles are impossible to fulfil on one's own.

To understand the essence of the Christian Gospel we have to look further. Look at:

Romans 7:14–25

● *Here St Paul affirms that obedience to the demands of the Jewish Law (Torah) is admirable, with all its moral and religious requirements, but the problem is that human nature is incapable of keeping that Law. In a sense, therefore, merely to set out what God asks of us is not 'good news' at all, but bad news, because it means that God is asking us to live on a level which is impossible for us to achieve.*

Look also at:

Galatians 3:23–25

● *In this brief passage Paul says that the Law was an interim measure on God's part, to keep people in check until the coming of Christ, who would make the Law unnecessary because it would then be superseded by faith.*

Thus the Gospel or 'good news' of the Christian religion is not so much a declaration of what we have to do to please God, but more an announcement that the power or strength to do it is now available.

In the New Testament, which is of course our earliest evidence of what was first preached, it is clear that the Christian message (or 'kerygma', to give it its proper name) gradually developed from very basic beginnings. At first it was essentially a Jewish message, in the nature of an announcement that the expected Messiah had come in the person of Jesus of Nazareth. This Jesus was known to be the Messiah because his resurrection from the grave had authenticated his identity. The ancient prophecies have been fulfilled, and the 'new age' of the Messiah has arrived.

Much of the teaching of St Paul is along these lines, though we have to be careful not to assume that his message was identical to that being preached by the Apostles. There were always differences of emphasis in what they said and how they said it.

The late Professor C. H. Dodd, one of the most important British theologians of the twentieth century, gave the following outline of the early preaching of St Paul:

'The prophecies are fulfilled, and the new Age is inaugurated by the coming of Christ. He was born of the seed of David. He died according to the Scriptures, to deliver us out of the present evil age. He was buried. He rose on the third day according to the Scriptures. He is exalted at the right hand of God, as Son of God and Lord of quick (i.e. "living") and dead. He will come again as Judge and Saviour of men.'

This differs in some respects from the content of what was preached by the Apostles who were resident in Jerusalem and

33

remained more closely aligned with the Jewish faith. They did not refer to Jesus as 'Son of God', but preferred to use Old Testament terms such as 'Servant of God'. Nor did they specifically claim that Jesus died 'for our sins', though we can take it that they expected forgiveness to be one of the fruits of the Messiah's coming. Otherwise, the preaching of St Paul was generally in line with what the Apostles were proclaiming.

One of the most striking features of the early preaching was its stress upon the idea that the 'Kingdom of God' had arrived, inaugurated by the life, death and resurrection of Jesus. This Kingdom, though not yet fully realised, was now in being, and would be finally manifested at the return of Christ. The preaching of the 'Kingdom' was not simply an element in the early Church's message: it was, according to the Gospel tradition, central to what Jesus himself had said during his own ministry. Look at:

Mark 1:14–15

● *These brief words summarise the message of Jesus himself, though we have to allow for the possibility that Mark may have 'read back' the early preaching and placed it on the lips of Jesus. However, it seems clear that Jesus himself was conscious that a new era had dawned, and that the Kingdom (or more accurately the 'kingly rule') of God had begun.*

The Gospel in the Gentile world

Preaching that the Messiah had come, and that the expected 'new age' had dawned, was meaningful to Jews because their own traditions and expectations provided the context for such a message. But would that proclamation make sense or have any relevance to people who were not Jewish? Would they even understand it, let alone accept it? Would they have to begin with a kind of 'crash course' in Judaism before they could make sense of the Christian Gospel? This was a real problem facing the early preachers, and we can see in the New

Testament how it was sometimes thought necessary to preface the preaching with a run-through of Jewish religious history (see, for example, Acts 2:14–36). But St Paul, who held to the view that the Gospel was for everyone and not for the Jews alone, introduced his preaching by appealing to the universal need for divine intervention (see Romans 1:18ff), and sought to put the Jews into that universal context. He used different images to express the nature of the Gospel, referring to the work of Christ as 'reconciling God with mankind'. Look at the following passage:

II Corinthians 18–19

● *Here Paul lays his stress upon the work of God as bringing people back into fellowship with himself, and refers to the Gospel as 'the message of reconciliation'.*

Sometimes Paul uses his Jewish traditions in a new way, for example when he used the event of the Exodus from Egypt as a basis for his idea that the Gospel was about God 'setting people free' from slavery:

Romans 8:1–17

● *In this passage Paul says that God's saving act has been to set people free from their own 'lower nature', and thus he is using language that would be intelligible both to Jews and also to Gentiles.*

As the Christian Church spread, and gradually broke away from its Jewish origins, the essence of the 'kerygma' became more diffused. The appeal to ancient prophecy gave way to arguments based on reason and common experience, and we can find many instances of attempts to win converts, not through proclamation but through rational persuasion and through practical demonstrations of the truth of the Gospel. The Church began to 'preach by example', using what is sometimes called 'the language of love' to break through national and racial barriers. This was based upon the principle that the 'word' was most effective when it 'became flesh'.

DISCUSSION POINTS

1. Is Christian preaching intelligible to people who have no background in religious thinking? Does it require some awareness of Biblical ideas?

2. Does a 'Gospel' about being set free from slavery have any relevance in today's world? Are people generally aware of being enslaved to anything at all? Can you think of examples of modern forms of slavery, from which the Christian Gospel might offer release?

3. Is it sufficient to present Christianity as a 'way of life'?

4. Has the Church been right to leave behind the 'Messianic' message, and to concentrate upon proclaiming its message by deeds rather than words?

5. In what sense can it be said that Christianity offers a Gospel of reconciliation, especially when there is division and disunity within the Church itself?

<table>
<tr><td>

7

</td><td>

The Christian Life

</td></tr>
</table>

It has often been said of the Jewish religion that it is not really a religion at all, but a way of life. The same could also be said of Christianity, because there has always been a very close connection made between what Christians believe and what they actually do. Belief and deed go together. St Paul constantly stressed this in his letters to the churches which he founded or visited. Look at the following passage:

I Corinthians 6:19–20

● *Paul makes the point that the human body has become the place where God's Holy Spirit now dwells, and therefore it is in the use of the body that God is to be honoured. Worship is inextricably bound up with behaviour.*

Look also at:

Romans 6:9–14

● *Once again, Paul links the Gospel with life. If Christians really have been raised to a new kind of life through the work of Christ, it must follow that they put themselves completely at God's disposal as 'implements for doing right'.*

The letter of James echoes this, though in a somewhat different way. Martin Luther described this particular document as 'an epistle of straw' because he found very little profound theology in it; but it stands as further evidence that early Christians were intent upon showing that what they believed must determine and shape what they did. Look at:

James 1:22–25

● *The point here is obvious. The Christian Gospel is not merely a set of principles, nor is it a theory to think about. It is a call to action. Belief without corresponding behaviour is empty.*

In the world but not of it

Although Christians believe that Christ has rescued them from slavery to the world, they still have to live within it. Their humanity may have been transformed, but they remain human just the same. So how does a Christian give expression to that transformed life? From very early times there have been some Christians who have felt that in order to give themselves up to the proper worship and service of God they must withdraw from worldly affairs and live out their lives in separation from everyday society. This was the impetus which sent many of them into the monastic life. Some took the principle so far that they became hermits – a word which is derived from a Greek term meaning 'desert'. At first they were found in considerable numbers in Egypt, where the 'eremitical' way of life became very popular. In due course, however, the custom lost its appeal, especially in the western Church, though it is still retained to some extent in such religious orders as the Carthusians and the Carmelites. Other Christians, who could not bring themselves to spend their time in complete isolation, went instead into religious communities, where they did not live in isolation but were still cut off from secular life. These have become known as 'coenobites', from Greek words meaning 'living a common life'.

The Christian within society

While it is true that many other religions have their monastic orders (for example, Buddhism), on the whole Christianity has not been entirely comfortable with this way of giving expression to the religious life. The great majority of Christians have tried instead to remain within ordinary secular society, believing that this is where their faith must be lived out. They are 'in the world, though not of it' (compare John 17:11–19). This has meant working out for themselves what it is that differentiates a Christian from anyone else, and three answers in particular have been found. First, Christians have adopted a different attitude towards God. Second, they have taken up a different attitude towards themselves. Third, they have taken a different attitude towards other people. We can look at each of these in turn.

THE CHRISTIAN ATTITUDE TOWARDS GOD:
For a Christian, as distinct from secular society, God is the focus of life and gives purpose to all that is done. This means that every action is seen as a part of one's worship. Every deed ought to be measured in terms of its compatibility with God's perceived will. In order to sustain this and keep the vision clearly in mind, a Christian feels the need to be 'fed from the roots of faith' at frequent intervals, and this is the reason why it is important for a Christian to be a part of a worshipping community (the Church), with direct access to the sources of spiritual nourishment. It is this God-consciousness which distinguishes a Christian from a humanist or a good atheist, because it determines the orientation of his or her entire life.

THE CHRISTIAN ATTITUDE TOWARDS ONESELF:
It is also a Christian principle that 'self' must come last rather than first. This is sometimes referred to as self-denial, though we have to make a distinction between this and the practice of self-mortification. This term was used to signify the once-common practice of 'killing' or 'deadening' the body by means of ascetic behaviour such as deliberately going without food or the self-infliction of physical pain and discomfort. This is rarely found in Christian practice nowadays, except in largely symbolic ways in certain monastic orders. The more common interpretation of this principle, particularly in everyday life, is that of being unselfish and humble. For a Christian it matters

that self-respect is maintained, but this is distinguished from self-aggrandisement and personal ambition.

THE CHRISTIAN ATTITUDE TOWARDS OTHER PEOPLE:
A Christian insists that no distinction is to be made between friend and enemy, rich and poor, old and young, friend and stranger. All alike are to be served in Christ's name, following the example set by Christ during his own ministry. The principle here is that of AGAPE ('love') – a word which goes far beyond ordinary usages. It involves giving without wanting anything back in return. Other people are regarded as brothers and sisters, regardless of who they are or what their religion might be. A Christian considers that the service of other people is also the service of God.

Unlike other religions, there are no hard and fast rules governing the Christian life. Islam, which numerically is probably the second largest religion in the world next to Christianity, sets out a very careful blueprint for its followers, making it clear what is considered to be acceptable behaviour and what is not. Christianity, on the other hand, gives its followers one simple principle, which is that of LOVE, and makes it clear that everything else follows naturally from this. St Augustine once offered the advice 'Love God, and then do as you like'. Because of this approach, which derives from the idea that the 'law' has been rendered obsolete by the grace of Christ, it is left to individual Christians to work out for themselves what is the proper course of action in any given set of circumstances. There are examples given, both in the teachings of Jesus and in the advice of St Paul, but these are illustrative of the central principle, rather than legalistic directives. Look at the following passage:

Matthew 5:38–6:18

● *This is a part of Christ's 'sermon on the mount', in which Matthew sums up the ethical teachings of Jesus. They are set out in a style suggestive of the giving of the Ten Commandments by Moses, but it is clear that this is not only a new law – it is also a new 'kind' of law.*

It is the continuing responsibility of Christians in every age and in every new set of circumstances to apply the principle of self-giving love, and this is possible only for those who live within the fellowship of faith and have access to its resources.

DISCUSSION POINTS

1. Is St Augustine's advice ('Love God, and do as you like') a sound Christian principle? Or is it dangerous?

2. Is the monastic life the ideal for all Christians?

3. What might a Christian make of the principle that 'charity begins at home'?

4. Are there any areas of life in which it is impossible to establish the Christian ideal? What about homosexuality, or pacifism, or abortion? Is there an obvious Christian attitude to take in such matters?

5. Does self-denial imply joylessness?

6. Does one have to go to church to be a Christian? Can the Christian life be separated from life in 'the body of Christ'?

7. Does someone have to be a Christian to be good?

8. Can a Christian sin in private, if 'no-one else gets hurt'?

9. It is sometimes said that a Christian should not adopt a 'holier than thou' attitude towards other people: but is it not true that a Christian really is holier than a non-Christian?

10. What do you understand by Christian love, as distinct from any other kind?

8 | Spreading the Gospel

Christianity is one of the world's 'missionary' faiths, in that it is committed to the task of spreading its teachings into every corner of the world. Not all religions do this. Judaism, for example, is not a missionary faith in that sense; Jews regard themselves as having been chosen by God, and their responsibility is to respond to that calling rather than to extend it further. Islam, on the other hand, like Christianity, is very much concerned with missionary activity and seeks to become worldwide and all-embracing. Thus there is an element of rivalry or competitiveness here, which has to be taken seriously. Historically, the period of the Crusades (11th to the 13th centuries) was a time when Christians engaged in military onslaughts to take back possession of the Holy Land from Islam. It was not a period of which the Christian Church has been proud, and it illustrates how easily the quest for 'souls' can turn into a battle for territory.

According to the Gospel of Matthew, it was the clear intention of Jesus that his followers should spread their faith and make converts. Look at:

Matthew 28:16–20

● *This passage has been the subject of considerable debate, but it clearly reflects the early Christian conviction that the Gospel was not to be restricted only to Jews. Whether Jesus could actually have used the words about baptising in the name of the Trinity is certainly questionable, but there can be no doubt at all that from a very early stage in the life of the Christian Church there was a strong missionary impulse.*

The task of spreading the Gospel was pioneered by St Paul,

himself a converted Jew. Unlike the other Apostles, he was not only willing but actually eager to spread Christianity into the Gentile world, where it took root and gradually lost some of its Jewish characteristics. It effectively became a world religion rather than a national faith.

However, the transition was far from easy. It was not only a matter of dealing with active hostility and persecution, severe as that was: more subtly it was a matter of finding new ways of presenting the Christian message to people who had no understanding of its origins or its background. New recruits to the Church frequently brought with them their old ideas and practices, and there was a constant danger that the original Gospel would become diffused and even lost altogether. There were language difficulties, cultural problems, and organisational complexities arising from a need to prevent things from getting out of control. Many of the divisions which have arisen within the Church have their roots in these issues.

Traditionalism in the Church

Right from the beginning of the Church's history there have been those who have feared that, in the enthusiasm to win converts or to present an acceptable public image, some of the essentials of the faith might be sacrificed. We can see this in the activities of Jewish Christians in the first century. They wanted to ensure that the traditional customs of Judaism were retained in the emerging churches, and tried to pull new Christians back towards the 'old ways'. Look at the following:

Galatians 3:1–14

● *Here, St Paul is writing sternly to a new congregation which is being encouraged to go backwards rather than forwards. He reminds them that they have left their Jewish ways behind, and cannot return to the practices of their traditional faith. He invites them to look again at their old teachings, and accept that things have moved on.*

43

Yet the spirit of traditionalism, if it has held things back in some respects, has also served to prevent the Church from rushing headlong into uncharted territory and untried practices. There has always been a need for the leaders of the Church to maintain a careful balance between going too fast and not going anywhere at all.

The ebb and flow of missionary activity

It has to be admitted that the missionary zeal of the Church, while continually present, has often waned. Once established as the 'official' religion of the Roman Empire there was a detectable slackening of interest in spreading the Gospel, because people were voluntarily joining the Church for social reasons. Yet it has always been acknowledged that it is of the essence of Christianity to reach out to others, and there have been 'spurts' of enthusiasm for doing this. In the Middle Ages there were concerted efforts to win over the untouched tribal groups of Europe, and the Crusades (despite their obvious faults) were founded upon a desire to spread Christianity among Muslims. Missionary work extended into India and China, but not always with resounding success. At the time of the Reformation this missionary endeavour again slackened because the Church was otherwise engaged in sorting out its own internal disputes. Then, especially from the nineteenth century, there came a resurgence of missionary concern, with the founding of societies committed to taking the Gospel overseas.

This involvement in 'foreign' missions was counterbalanced by a growing concern for the social needs here in Britain, and various attempts were made to deal with such problems as poverty and drunkenness by 'missions to the poor'. It was becoming evident that the concept of spreading the Gospel was changing from one of mere recruitment to one of service.

In recent times this change of approach and attitude has

become more evident, and the contemporary missionary is no longer quite like his predecessors. The emphasis is now much more upon planting a Christian 'presence' than upon opening up new churches, and it is becoming normal for the Church to involve itself more directly in social projects such as teaching people how to set up and run their own communities in a Christian way. Teachers, technicians, doctors and engineers now swell the ranks of missionary endeavour, and there is a much greater respect being paid to the indigenous cultures of the people to whom the Church is reaching out. There have been points at which the Church has found itself embroiled in political and commercial issues, but this is inevitable if it is to be true to its commitment to go right to the heart of human society.

Mission in the local church

Within the life of local congregations, it has to be admitted that there has not always been a great deal of evidence of successful 'outreach'. With some notable exceptions, the denominations have been largely content to invite people in, rather than to go out and get them. There have been numerous campaigns and evangelistic crusades up and down the land, and alongside these there are the continuing activities of smaller groups such as seaside missions to holidaymakers; yet on the whole there is an evident reluctance – bordering upon embarrassment – among the mainstream denominations to treat the spreading of the Gospel as a natural and on-going aspect of their life. Churches have tended to cater for the needs of their own members rather than to look outwards at the non-churchgoers.

Various reasons for this have been suggested – not the least being that the 'average Christian' is not sufficiently well-versed in the faith to feel qualified to talk about it to others. Another suggestion is that the Church has generally lagged behind in developing a 'language' which it can use to persuade the unbeliever; it has tended to stay with archaic and unintelligible jargon which is left over from the past. Related to this is the complaint that the Church is generally out of touch with contemporary events and attitudes, and is perceived as being too 'holy' to have much relevance to ordinary needs. Yet it is also recognised that if the Church becomes too involved in the world it is in danger of compromising itself and becoming indistinguishable from those it seeks to serve. Look at the following passage:

II Corinthians 6:3-13

● *Here, St Paul summarises his own missionary approach. He tries to work through personal example as well as through proclamation. He tries to avoid giving offence, yet at the same time he stands up for what he believes, and is willing to put up with persecution and humiliation as a part of the price that has to be paid. All he asks is that people will be prepared to listen to him.*

DISCUSSION POINTS

1. In our contemporary open-minded and multi-faith society, ought Christians to stop trying to recruit people into the Church, and leave them to follow their own paths in matters of religion?

2. Is mission the same thing as service?

3. Does the extending of the Church necessarily involve change?

4. How far can the Church become involved in secular affairs, without compromising its own principles?

5. Missionary activity has sometimes resulted in the break-up of families and even of whole communities. Is this justified?

6. Does the modern world offer the Church any new ways of spreading the Gospel?

9	**What is a Church?**

The word 'Church'

The English word 'church' comes from a Greek term ('kyriakon') which originally signified something which belonged to God, and at first it was used to denote a building which was dedicated to Christian worship. However, there was another Greek word ('ekklesia'), which literally meant 'called out' or 'separated', and this was used to refer to an assembly of people who had been specially appointed or selected for positions of responsibility. This latter word appears in the Greek translation of the Old Testament, where it denotes the 'assembly' of the Hebrew people, and it was particularly appropriate as a term to represent God's 'Chosen People'.

Today, the word 'church' is used to refer both to a building in which Christians meet, and also to the actual congregation or fellowship itself. It is this latter sense which is to occupy us in this particular study.

What constitutes a Christian Church?

This is a very difficult question to answer, although on the surface it looks quite straightforward. First, can we properly speak of 'a' Christian church, or is it more accurate to speak of 'the' Christian Church (with a capital 'C')? If we choose the former, it suggests that there are many churches, and of course this is indeed true in the sense that there are many different branches or denominations, all calling themselves churches, but clearly different from each other in certain important respects. In view of this, in what sense is it possible to speak at all of 'the' Christian Church in an all-embracing sense? What is it that holds them all together in their tremendous variety, and gives them a common nature?

Essentially 'the' Church (in all its forms) regards itself as the body or presence of Christ on earth. It would be going too far to think of it as an extension of the incarnation, because that would be to attribute to it a perfection which it evidently does not possess; nevertheless, it sees itself as continuing Christ's work, and as being 'empowered' by him to further the establishment of his kingdom on earth.

Look at the following passage:

I Corinthians 12:12–31

● *In this passage St Paul describes the nature not only of one particular Christian congregation, but of all such fellowships. He uses the analogy of a human body to illustrate the relation of the diverse parts of the body to the whole.*

It seems, then, that diversity (or, as some would prefer, variety) is one of the characteristics of the Christian Church, but that diversity is held together in a special kind of unity which derives from its head – Jesus Christ. Uniformity and unity are not the same thing.

It would also appear from the evidence of the New Testament that, from the outset, the Christian Church was conscious of being the 'New Israel', in that it represented God's 'chosen people' called out from the world in order to serve it. Look at the following passage:

I Peter 2:9–10

● *This passage accurately reflects the way in which the early Christians saw themselves in relation to the world around them, especially in their early days when they were still closely linked with Judaism. They were conscious of having been taken by God, in the manner of the Old Testament prophets. It is evident that they did not think of themselves as a group of 'volunteers'.*

As the Church spread into the western world, both through missionary endeavour and as a consequence of the destruction of Jerusalem in AD 70, it gradually disconnected itself from mainstream Judaism, and its physical centre came to be established in Rome – the capital city of the Roman Empire. It took on some of the characteristics of an Empire in itself, especially in its efforts to maintain peace and stability within its own ranks. Its leadership eventually came from the head of the church in Rome, giving rise to what became known as Roman Catholicism.

The Great Schism of the 11th century produced a divided Church, split into East and West, with each branch claiming to be faithful to its apostolic beginnings and accusing the other of being schismatic. Then the Reformation of the 16th century brought further fragmentation into the western Church. Here, the issue was the fundamental question of authority: how was Christ's lordship over his Church to be exercised in practice? Over against the Roman Catholic position stood the Reformers, who generally held to the view that the final authority in all matters of Christian life was that of the Scriptures, rightly interpreted through the Holy Spirit.

It is clear that what was emerging out of these great changes was a 'theology of the Church' – that is to say, a developing understanding of the Church's inner nature, as distinct from its organisation. Serious questions had to be faced, about the true seat of government within the Church, the importance of tradition and of the Sacraments, the place of the laity, the authority of the priesthood, and even about whether priests were necessary at all. The quest was for a recovery of the 'Church principle', which, it was at first believed, could be identified through careful study of the Apostolic beginnings. When it became evident that the New Testament did not (and

49

could not) furnish a blueprint for Church organisation, the search was re-directed towards establishing a common understanding of how the unity of Christ could be expressed in the diversity of his 'body'.

The rise of the Ecumenical Movement has given new impetus to this quest, with the various denominations and branches of the Church now showing a greater readiness to share their insights with one another. Topic 20 in this Study Guide takes this particular matter further, and groups may wish to turn to it immediately after this one.

DISCUSSION POINTS

1. **Can a group of committed Christians constitute a 'church', while remaining independent of all other congregations? What conditions would they have to fulfil in order to become a genuine church?**

2. **What are the requirements and qualifications for membership of the Christian Church?**

3. **Consider the claim that 'a church is more like a hospital for sinners than a club for saints'.**

4. **Does someone have to 'go to church' in order to be a Christian?**

5. **Accepting that Christ is the true Head of the Church, how is his authority best exercised?**

6. **If the Church is to be understood as the Body of Christ, must it ultimately die?**

7. **In view of the divisions within Christendom, can we still honestly claim that 'the Church' exists?**

8. **If Scripture is to be the ultimate authority in the life of the Church, what guarantees are there that it is 'rightly interpreted'?**

9. **Was the Christian religion spoiled when it was turned into an institution, as distinct from a way of life?**

10. **How can we tell whether a church is alive or dead?**

10 | Christian Baptism

Ever since the beginning of Christian history, Baptism has been recognised as the mode of entry into membership of the Church. The word itself is not particularly significant: it comes from a Greek term which meant simply 'to dip in water'.

Christian Baptism is also regarded as one of the two great 'Dominical' sacraments of the Church, the other being Holy Communion. These are singled out because according to the New Testament they were specifically ordained by Jesus himself as practices which his followers should repeat (see Matthew 28:19 and I Corinthians 11:23–26).

It has often been mistakenly thought that Jesus himself underwent Christian Baptism at the hands of John the Baptist. This, however, is not the case: Christian Baptism did not exist at that time, and what Jesus really received was a form of Jewish baptism intended to prepare Jews to receive the expected Messiah and the judgement that he was thought to bring. Although Christian Baptism bears outward similarities to that ritual, it really has its origins in Jesus' own death and resurrection.

What does Christian Baptism mean?

The clearest exposition of the meaning of Christian Baptism is given by St Paul, in his letter to the Romans. Look at this passage:

Romans 6:1–11

● *Paul explains to the Christians in Rome that through Baptism they have 'died to sin'. The sacrament brought*

*them into union with Christ, and by it they participated in
his death. Thus they are enabled to enter the new life, made
possible by Christ's resurrection.*

Christian Baptism is therefore a sacramental 'dying' – and
some have compared it to drowning, linking it with the Old
Testament story of the great flood in which sinful humanity
died and righteousness (represented by Noah and his family)
emerged triumphant. To a lesser degree it can also be likened
to the rituals of 'washing' which could be found both in
earlier Judaism and in other religions.

Unlike the sacrament of Holy Communion, Christian Baptism
is a once-for-all action. The simple explanation for this is that
whereas people have to eat and drink frequently in order to
replenish their strength and stay alive, they die only once. In
the early Church it was considered wrong to be baptised a
second time, and the writer of the letter to the Hebrews is in
all probability referring to this in the following passage:

Hebrews 5:4–8

● *Although the word 'baptism' is not used in this passage,
nevertheless there are clear hints of it in the use of the word
'enlightened' and the following reference to sharing in the
Holy Spirit. The analogy of rainwater falling upon the
earth is also significant, as is the statement that a 'second
chance' will mean crucifying Christ for a second time.*

If we can judge from the evidence of the New Testament,
Baptism was administered first to converts (who would generally be adult believers) and then to their families. It is not
possible to determine exactly how the ritual was carried out,
though it has been claimed that both sprinkling with water
from a small container and total immersion (in a large font or
a river) were practised.

However, the on-going debate within the Christian Church
has not really focussed mainly upon the distinction between

sprinkling and total immersion; rather, it has been concerned with the question of whether Baptism ought to be offered only to professing believers, or whether it is an 'open' sacrament which can affect even those who are unable to make that prior confession of faith. Obviously, the custom of Infant Baptism comes into this second category, because a baby cannot make any sort of personal promise or acknowledgement, and has to rely upon the faith of the parents until maturity is reached.

The rite of Confirmation (or 'Church Membership' as it is known in some denominations) represents the 'second stage' of Infant Baptism, in that it affords an opportunity for someone who was baptised in infancy to confirm the promises originally made on his or her behalf. It is in itself an acknowledgement that the effectiveness of Baptism does depend upon the faith of the recipient.

Christening

It has become customary to refer to Christian Baptism as 'Christening', and at one level this is a perfectly acceptable term to use, since it means 'to make Christ's own'. But at another level it marks a common misconception of what Baptism is all about, since it is often treated as a social convention or as a simple naming ceremony. Large numbers of parents request 'Christening' for their children without any awareness of what it implies, and without any intention of bringing up their own child in the fellowship of the Church. Some ministers and clergy insist that certain conditions are met before they will agree to perform these ceremonies, some refuse to perform them at all, and some practise what has come to be called 'indiscriminate Baptism' on the ground that it provides a point of contact with the family, which can then be followed up later.

The Name of the Trinity

According to the command of Jesus in Matthew's Gospel, Baptism should be 'in the name of the Father, and of the Son, and of the Holy Spirit', and this is the formula which is generally used. Because this is a practice which transcends denominational barriers, it is usual (though not universal) for the various branches of the Church to accept the validity of a Baptism which was carried out in a different church. The only major exception to this is the Baptist churches, which hold to the principle that true Baptism can be administered only to believers, and has no meaning for infants. In these churches, the ceremony involves the total immersion of the candidate in water, thus representing in very dramatic form the idea of 'going down into the water' in order to rise again to a new life in Christ.

DISCUSSION POINTS

1. Is Christian Baptism only a symbolic act of initiation, or does it have some deeper significance?
2. If Christ died for all, regardless of their age or their ability to understand, does it not follow that Christian Baptism should be made openly available to everyone without condition?
3. Should Christian Baptisms be performed in the presence of the whole congregation, or can the sacrament be administered in private?
4. What is the role of the church-family in the Baptism of any particular individual?
5. Is Infant Baptism still meaningful if it is not followed by Confirmation?
6. If someone has never been baptised, is he/she a true Christian?

<table>
<tr><td>**11**</td><td># Holy Communion</td></tr>
</table>

This Sacrament is known under several different names. It is often referred to as the EUCHARIST, from a Greek word meaning 'thanksgiving'. In the Roman Catholic Church it is called the MASS, and in many Protestant churches it is called the LORD'S SUPPER, from John Wycliffe's English version of the New Testament (I Corinthians 11:20). However, the general term HOLY COMMUNION is now widely used throughout many branches of the Church, and we will use it throughout this study.

The origin of the Sacrament

The New Testament provides us with several accounts of the last supper which Jesus shared with his disciples, immediately before his arrest and trial. The earliest is almost certainly that provided by St Paul. Look at:

I Corinthians 11:23–26

● *In this description Paul records what he refers to as a 'tradition' which he says he received directly from the Lord himself, although it is not entirely clear what he means by this. Evidently Jesus used the elements of bread and wine to signify his impending death, and made a direct link between the wine and the 'new covenant' which the prophet Jeremiah had promised in Old Testament times (see Jeremiah 31:31–34).*

Another very early account is provided by St Mark in his Gospel. Look at:

Mark 14:22–25

● *Mark's version of what happened is slightly different from that of Paul. A significant omission is the reference to the perpetuation of the meal as a 'memorial' – something which appears twice in Paul's account.*

Both St Matthew and St Luke include descriptions of the supper in their Gospels (Matthew 26:26f and Luke 22:14f). These seem to have been drawn from Mark's earlier account, although that given by Luke is complicated by the fact that there are some ancient manuscript versions of his Gospel in which there are significant variations in the text. Groups may wish to make detailed comparisons here.

Was the Last Supper a Jewish Passover meal?

Most scholars accept that the original supper which Jesus shared with his disciples was the traditional Passover meal of the Jews. This is supported by the fact that, according to Mark's Gospel (Mark 14:12f), it is explicitly stated that this was the case. There has been some debate over the years concerning whether what happened at the meal was in line with traditional Jewish customs, but we can take it that the link with the Passover is strongly made – in which case it seems reasonable to use Passover theology in order to understand what the meal meant. It was regarded as a sacrificial meal, celebrated as a family occasion, and originally it included the eating of a lamb which had been sacrificed in the Temple and then taken home by the worshippers. No doubt this tradition was very much in the minds of early Jewish Christians, who came to see Jesus as the new 'Paschal Lamb' sacrificed on their behalf; this is borne out by Paul in his letter to the Corinthians (I Corinthians 5:7).

The family meal

The fact that this was a home-based meal, in which all the

members of the family unit came together, has given rise to a further element in the interpretation of the supper. There can be no doubt that it owes much to the time-honoured custom of expressing family unity by eating and drinking together around the family table. It has always been true, especially in the eastern world, that by offering someone hospitality in one's own home, alongside the members of one's family, a deep bond is created. A stranger is thereby made to feel 'at home', and is welcomed into the family unit. Our word COMPANION reflects this same idea: it comes from the Latin words 'com' ('with') and 'panis' ('bread'), suggesting the deepening of friendships by the sharing of a fellowship meal.

Teachings about the meaning of Holy Communion

There have been differences of opinion within the Church about the true meaning of the sacrament of Holy Communion. Sometimes these were little more than differences of emphasis, but at other times they became very serious rifts. From the beginning it has been accepted that in some way the eating of the bread and the drinking of the wine serve to communicate or convey the body and blood of Christ to the worshipper, but the precise means by which this happens is not always agreed.

The doctrine of TRANSUBSTANTIATION, characteristic of the Roman Catholic Church, affirms that the elements of bread and wine actually become the body and blood of Christ, thus crossing from one 'substance' to another, leaving behind only their appearances (or 'accidents'). The eastern churches hold much the same doctrine, but prefer to use the word METOUSIOSIS. Protestant churches, since the Reformation, have largely rejected this doctrine. Martin Luther attempted to tread a middle path by proposing a view of CONSUBSTANTIA-TION, meaning that after the bread and wine had been consecrated they conveyed the body and blood of Christ to the worshipper but did not themselves change in nature, remaining as they were but existing together with Christ's presence. The Swiss reformer Ulrich Zwingli strongly supported the belief that the bread and wine were no more than symbols of Christ's physical presence, and his ideas created deep divisions within the Protestant ranks. These different ideas have somehow managed to co-exist within the contemporary Church, and it has been said that the ambiguous language of the Anglican Book of Common Prayer was actually intended to allow this to happen.

Differences in practice

The Roman Catholic Church and the Anglican Church have retained the custom of celebrating Holy Communion on an altar, with a priest officiating. In these churches the worshippers leave their seats and approach the altar rail to receive the elements from the priest's hands. But in the Free Church tradition the altar has gone, and in its place stands a Communion Table, devoid of candles and usually surrounded by chairs. The minister (who is not a priest) or some other duly-appointed person officiates, and in many of these churches the worshippers remain in their places, so that the bread and wine can be brought to them individually. Although there is often a common chalice or cup in evidence, it is from tiny individual glasses that the worshippers drink the wine, consuming it simultaneously in order to demonstrate their unity in Christ.

These variations in practice are not accidental: they reflect quite deep differences of understanding concerning the theology of the sacrament of Holy Communion. There are further differences of opinion about whether the sacrament should be 'opened up' to all who wish to participate in it, or whether it should be for church members only – that is, for those who have actually been confirmed or have joined the church by profession of their personal faith. Yet another question, currently exercising the minds of church leaders of many denominations, is that of whether it is proper to allow young children to share in the 'family meal' of the church – especially in these days when 'family worship' is being encouraged.

It is seen by many as one of the ironies of Christian church life that the sacrament which is, above all, supposed to demonstrate the unity of the body of Christ in worship is the very one which holds them apart in practice.

DISCUSSION POINTS

1. Is it essential for the Christian Church to have only one interpretation of the meaning of Holy Communion?

2. Does it matter who officiates at the sacrament of Holy Communion? Must it always be a priest, or even a male priest?

3. Should Holy Communion be celebrated frequently, or is once a month sufficient?

4. Does it matter whether the wine used in Communion services is alcoholic or not? And should the bread be in any way special?

5. Do you agree with opening up the sacrament of Holy Communion to anyone who sincerely wishes to participate, or should it be reserved for church members only?

6. In what sense do the elements of bread and wine convey the body and blood of Christ to the worshipper?

7. Is Holy Communion simply a memorial service?

8. Is there any essential difference between an altar and a Communion Table?

12	**Christian Worship**

It is true, of course, that the worship of God involves the whole of a Christian's life. Every action, every thought, and every word should be directed towards honouring God. However, while giving due weight to this, it is also true that there are occasions when a Christian feels the need to step back from that everyday life and spend time in concentrated acts of worship; mundane matters can temporarily be put to one side and the focus of the worshipper's attention can be given to God alone. Conventionally (though not necessarily) these special times of worship are spent in the company of others, because it is traditional for Christians to meet together for this purpose. It has always been acknowledged that Christian worship is most fully expressed in a community context. We can see evidence of this in the New Testament:

Acts 2:42–47

● *Here, St Luke records the custom of the earliest Christians, laying stress upon the fact that their life was corporate in both worship and work. They were drawn together by their common faith into a common life.*

At first they met in one another's houses, but as time passed it became usual to set aside special buildings which – like the Jewish Temple and then the synagogues – were used for worship. They were also frequently used for study and for meetings of various kinds. The central act of corporate worship was the Eucharist (Holy Communion), but closely associated with it in very early times was a kind of fellowship meal generally known as the AGAPE. This was sometimes known as a 'love-feast'. However, the fellowship meal gradually dropped out of favour: St Augustine (AD 354–430) noted that it had turned into little more than a charity supper.

The shape of corporate worship

Because early Christian worship was corporate rather than individual it became organised, though much of the spontaneity was retained. We can catch a glimpse of what sometimes happened at these services: look at the following passage:

I Corinthians 14:26–40

● *This passage has frequently been the cause of debate, in that Paul evidently regarded it as improper for women to speak out during corporate worship. But these words do reveal that the meetings were characterised by general participation, and apparently not dominated by one particular individual. The aim was to build up the fellowship, not to create confusion.*

From these early beginnings there gradually emerged a pattern of worship, often referred to as a (or 'the') LITURGY. This has been explained very precisely by Gregory Dix, a monk of Nashdom Abbey, in his definitive study of the development of the 'shape' of Christian worship:

' "Liturgy" is the name given ever since the days of the apostles of the act of taking part in the solemn corporate worship of God by the "priestly" society of Christians, who are "the Body of Christ, the church". "The Liturgy" is the term which covers generally all that worship which is officially organised by the church, and which is open to and offered by, or in the name of, all who are members of the church." (*The Shape of the Liturgy*), A. and C. Black, 1945, page 1.)

In all parts of the Christian Church there have been certain elements built into the Liturgy and regarded as necessary for a full 'diet' of worship. Apart from the central act of the Eucharist, which is covered in Topic 11, there have been prayers, readings from the Scriptures, hymns, and some kind of Christian instruction in the form of a sermon or homily. These have been carefully positioned in the order or pattern of worship, creating a sense that worship is a kind of conversation with God: he speaks to his people through the Scriptures, the Sacrament of Holy Communion, and through the sermon. The worshippers respond through their prayers, their hymns, and their attentive listening to God's word which comes to them through the words of the priest, minister or preacher. This dialogue takes a variety of forms, but the central purpose is always the same – that is, to enable Christians to draw upon God so that they can be renewed for their continuing discipleship.

Changing patterns of worship

With the passing of the years, certain changes and developments have taken place in Christian worship, and these are often a direct consequence of denominational standpoints. Sometimes the sermon has become the central feature, epitomised by the dominance of the pulpit in the furnishing and general architectural style of the building. Where this has happened, the congregation has found itself becoming more like an audience. At other times the altar has taken pride of place, standing higher than the congregation and demonstrating the centrality of the Sacrament of the Eucharist. In some churches the emphasis is placed upon music in worship, with the organ becoming a very significant feature. Over against this there have arisen Christian congregations who seek to express their worship of God in quietness – the Society of Friends(Quakers) are a good example of such an approach.

In some churches there has been an on-going debate about whether it is proper to include the taking of a collection within the act of worship. This has been defended by those who see it as a symbol of the worshippers' full commitment to God, and opposed by those who feel that it is an intrusion into what ought to be a spiritual activity. In much the same way there have also been arguments about the making of announcements concerning the church's weekly activities or forthcoming events; are these integral parts of the Christian life of the congregation, offered to God, or are they merely 'commercials' which break up the service and ruin the atmosphere?

Ideally, a service of worship should be a coherent activity in which all the differing elements combine together in harmony with each other. Those who lead public worship have often been heard to complain that they dislike the practice of inviting the congregation to sing their 'favourite' hymns, regardless of whether the sentiments (or even the theology) of those hymns are consistent with everything else that is being done. Others have called into question the practice of including a talk aimed specifically at the young children in the congregation, on the ground that this creates distinctions within what ought to be a unified gathering.

The most common complaint levelled against practically all the contemporary denominations (with a few exceptions, of course) is that their worship is generally dull. The exceptions are usually those churches in which music and drama have come into their own. However, the defenders of traditional patterns of worship often respond by pointing out that an act of worship is not intended to entertain the congregation, and certainly should not be confused with a religious concert. The 'enjoyment' of an act of worship is not the same as the pleasurable experience of spending an evening in a theatre. Nevertheless, there has always been a recognition, in all the denominations, that patterns of worship need to reflect changes in society, and this has been evidenced in such things as the introduction of new hymns and modern prayers couched in everyday language. The quest always is to balance the needs of the worshippers with the equally important need to retain a sense of what worship is about. The word 'worship' itself ('worthship') suggests the honouring of God, and anything that cheapens worship in pursuit of the aim of making it popular is likely to do more harm than good.

DISCUSSION POINTS

1. **How can worship be enlivened without destroying its dignity?**
2. **If all life ought to be worshipful, is corporate worship really necessary?**

3. How important is the sermon in an act of worship?

4. Is worship for beginners in the faith, or is it for those whose spiritual experience is advanced?

5. What are the right conditions for the worship of God?

6. Does spontaneity matter in Christian worship?

7. What makes a good prayer?

8. St Paul felt that speaking with tongues in corporate worship was not always helpful because it was hard to understand. Does this suggest anything about the use of symbolic actions in worship?

9. Can anyone lead worship? Is a leader even necessary?

10. Should the offering of money (the collection) be regarded as an act of worship?

13	**Christian Festivals**

Like other religions, Christianity has numerous special days in its yearly calendar. However, the various denominations differ in their celebration of them; some of the festivals are observed only in particular churches, being ignored altogether in others. Both the Roman Catholic and the Anglican churches provide lists of 'days of observance' for the guidance of their members, though this is not a common practice in the other branches of the western Church. For Roman Catholics, feast days which are of particular importance are known as 'Feasts of Obligation', and both the clergy and the ordinary church members are expected to observe them.

The observance of Sunday

The most obvious 'special day' in the Christian year is Sunday, which has always been regarded as a kind of weekly celebration of Easter. It is generally observed as a commemoration of the Resurrection of Christ, and counts as the first day of a new week – contrary to many secular calendars and diaries which treat Sunday as part of the weekend. It gradually replaced the Jewish Sabbath as a day of rest, but scholars have noted that it was the Roman Emperor Constantine who, in AD 321, laid down that Sunday should be a public holiday, and not the Church councils themselves. There is some evidence to suggest that Christians actually disliked the idea of doing nothing on this special day, feeling that it encouraged idleness. So, instead of placing their emphasis upon Sunday as a day of rest, Church leaders tried to impress upon Christians that it was to be 'kept holy' rather than kept empty of work.

Feast days

Apart from the celebration of Sunday, the Church has recognised two types of feast days. There are those which have a fixed place in the calendar, occurring on the same date each year ('Immovable Feasts'), and there are those which have variable dates ('Movable Feasts') because they derive from Jewish origins, where special days were associated with the timing of the full moon. Christmas is an example of an immovable feast, since it always occurs on the same day each year, while Easter is a movable feast because it changes annually – as also does Whitsun (Pentecost), which is linked with it. From time to time there have been attempts to fix the date of Easter in order to make the planning of the calendar more straightforward, but always without success.

The Christian calendar actually begins, not on January 1st, but on the first Sunday in Advent (the Sunday nearest to 30 November). From this point, each Sunday is used as a 'marker' to enable worshippers to follow the liturgical pattern. The two great feasts of Christmas and Easter are preceded by periods when Christians are encouraged to engage in preparation and discipline ('fasts'). Christmas is preceded by Advent (which has largely been neglected as a time of fasting), and Easter is preceded by Lent (where the custom of 'giving something up' has continued, though not always very strictly). Many of the other special days in the annual calendar have tended to pass without much notice being taken of them, especially in the Free Church tradition. Occasions such as Ascension Day and Trinity Sunday in particular have fallen prey to this, though they are more commonly observed in the Roman Catholic and Anglican churches.

'Unofficial' festivals and special days

A common tendency in recent times has been to add certain special days of a general nature to the calendar, which are linked, not with the life of Jesus or the great doctrines of the

Church, but with social concerns. We now encounter, for example, Christian Aid Sunday, Education Sunday, the Week of Prayer for Christian Unity, and numerous other occasions which are either nationally or locally observed. Church Anniversary Sundays are common, and one local church was even seen to be observing 'Minister's Birthday Sunday'.

One special celebration of this general sort has come to be looked upon as a major occasion in the church year, and that is Harvest Festival (or Harvest Thanksgiving). Although the Jewish year certainly recognises the religious importance of harvests, this has never been a true element in the Christian calendar. It is a sort of unofficial festival occasion, without a recognised date but usually falling somewhere in September or October, depending upon when the agricultural harvest is completed. The only formal link which traditional Christianity has made with Harvest thanksgiving was in mediaeval times: Lammas Day (1st August) was a time when bread from the newly-ripe corn was consecrated, but even this can hardly be regarded as the true forerunner of the now well-established festival, and in any case the old Lammas custom has virtually disappeared.

Another special day, which like Harvest has no true place in the Christian calendar, is Remembrance Sunday (the Sunday nearest to 11 November). It is used as an opportunity to think of those who gave their lives or who suffered in other ways during the major wars, and to contemplate the continuing importance of working for peace. This particular occasion is becoming increasingly controversial within Christendom. Some who hold strongly pacifist principles often see it as coming close to the glorification of war, and others object to it on the ground that Christians should try to concentrate on forgiving their enemies rather than upon raking over the past. Those who support it insist that it is wrong to forget those who have sacrificed their lives or their health for the sake of others, and that this remembrance should be embodied within their religious activities. They point out that it is customary to remember the suffering and death of Christ, who gave his life for others.

The purpose of festivals and special days

The setting aside of special days has always been a feature of world religions, and the Jewish-Christian tradition is by no means exceptional. Such days have been used for a variety of purposes. Some are simply anniversary occasions, when significant people or important events are consciously remembered. They help to ensure that the past is not forgotten. Others are times when the followers of a religion are called to take stock of themselves and their faith, stepping back from the routines of life to think about where they are going. One religion which is something of an exception to all this is Sikhism: the founder of the Sikhs (Guru Nanak) disliked the way in which religions tended to encourage the observance of special days, and tried to persuade his followers to simplify their practices because he felt that these many celebrations were becoming corrupted. He was not entirely successful in his protests, because modern Sikhs still have their special days including the celebration of Guru Nanak's own birthday; nevertheless, he did highlight an important point, which was that there can be a risk to genuine religion if celebrations are allowed to get out of hand. We can find a similar attitude in the Old Testament: look at:

Amos 5:21–27

● *This prophet of the 8th century* BC *was complaining that feasts and ceremonies had got in the way of sincere worship, and said that what God wanted was not special celebrations but justice and goodness.*

DISCUSSION POINTS

1. In what sense should Sunday be a special day for Christians? Is the idea of a day of rest compatible with Christian principles about avoiding idleness?

2. Have the Free Churches been right to ignore many of the feast days of the traditional Christian calendar?

3. In what ways might the disciplines of Advent and Lent be made relevant to contemporary Christian practice?

4. Is the modern tendency to introduce new special days justified? Has it got out of control?

5. Why, in your opinion, has Harvest Festival never been treated as an official Christian celebration?

6. Are the opponents of Remembrance Sunday right or wrong in their criticisms of it?

7. Is it true that the celebration of special days can distract Christians from the proper worship of God?

14 | The Bible and the Church

This study is not an exploration of the Bible as such, but rather is about its place in the life and worship of the Christian Church. It is often forgotten that the Bible was never intended to stand on its own, independently of the community which brought it into being. The modern fashion for studying the Bible in isolation from the Church, treating it as an example of ancient Middle Eastern religious literature, is dangerous: it obscures the fact that the Bible is a book of faith, intended for use within a worshipping community. To read it independently of its Church context is rather like trying to evaluate the worth of the telephone directory without having access to a telephone.

Modern scholarship has shown that the literature of the Bible, in both the Old and New Testaments, has been collected together as a kind of 'inspirational storehouse', from which worshippers can draw as they feel inclined. Taken as a whole, it reflects the many-sided life of a religious community of people, struggling to make sense of their experience and to understand what it is that God is saying to them. It also demonstrates the wide variety of ways in which God has been perceived, both by individuals and by whole groups.

Not all parts of the Bible are of equal value for Christian purposes. Some are of historical interest only, and can affect the life of the Church only in a very indirect way. The lists of names in the book of Numbers chapter 26, for instance, or the details of tribal movements in chapter 33, can hardly be described as spiritually nourishing. Furthermore, because the Biblical literature is extremely old it has to be recognised that some of the cultural attitudes reflected in it are inappropriate in the present century. Views about the place of women in society, for example, have to be seen in the light of the times when they were current. Conversely, there are many parts of the Bible which provide insights into matters which are time-less, and apply to all generations in all places. Even those Christians who attempt to hold to a fundamentalist or literalist position regarding the Bible have to admit that they do not make use of every single part of it. It is one of the tasks of the present-day Church to establish how much of the Biblical literature is meaningful and useful for modern Christians.

The Bible as the Church's ultimate authority

At the time of the Reformation, when there was a great deal of dispute about the seat of authority in the Christian Church, many people said that the Bible had to be regarded as the final arbiter in matters of faith. Martin Luther's supposed affirma-tion 'Here I stand: I can do no other!' (which he may not actually have said) referred to the Bible as the ultimate authority in the Church. The problem, however, was that of knowing whether the words of the Bible were being correctly interpreted or understood. It has always been very easy to indulge in the practice of 'text-swapping', playing off one Bible passage against another, in order to defend a particular point of view, and this is because the Bible is a diverse collection of writings and not a systematic directory of belief.

The Bible in Christian worship

If it is difficult to use the Bible as a reference book for doctrine, then it is much easier to use it as a source of inspiration, and this is what regularly happens in Christian worship. Week by week, preachers in churches of all kinds use the Bible as the basis for their sermons. Even though it is now rather less fashionable to preach from a specific text, the Bible still provides the themes for what is said in the pulpit and presented as the word of God to his people. As one theologian put it, 'if we do not always preach from the text, we certainly preach from the texture of the Scriptures'. Lectionaries, which essentially are systematic programmes of Biblical passages for the use of preachers throughout the Christian year, help to provide a structure which the Bible in itself does not give.

It is a normal (though not an inviolable) practice for churches to use the Old Testament and the New Testament in worship, with readings taken from both. The Old Testament passage will frequently serve to introduce the later reading from the New Testament, preparing the ground for it and illustrating the continuity of the theme or idea. However, it is not at all unusual to hear some Christians suggesting that the Old Testament is no longer relevant, and that it should not be read in churches. Some even go so far as to say that it reflects teachings which Jesus actually countermanded in his own sermons. It is certainly true that when the Christian religion moved out from Jewish territory into the western world, the Old Testament came to be less significant in missionary activity because the hearers were totally unfamiliar with its contents and the cultural environment out of which it had grown.

The Bible as a means of conversion

The emphasis upon the importance and the centrality of the Bible led to the idea that it could actually be a means of converting people to the Christian faith, independently of the Church which had brought it into being. This resulted in practices such as that of distributing free copies of the Bible to all who would receive them, of putting Bibles in hotel rooms, hospitals and prisons, and of insinuating copies of the Bible into countries where missionaries were not allowed entry. This has often been called into question as a proper way of using the Christian Scriptures. The perceived danger is that when the Bible is read without commentary or guidance it can very easily be misunderstood, resulting in the forming of unbalanced or even absurd ideas about what it actually means. This has proved to be true in some cases, because the growth of eccentric and heretical sects can often be traced back to someone who took the words of the Bible out of their proper context.

It was this kind of danger which caused the Church of earlier centuries to insist that the Bible should not be made too freely available. It was considered that the priests and other learned people of the Church ought to keep a tight hold of its interpretation, so that it would not fall into the hands of those who had no idea of how to read it. Even the business of translating the Bible into English was resisted on these same grounds. Today, however, copies of the Bible are readily available – and it is perhaps ironic that so many people who now own one do not actually look at it.

The Bible and the individual Christian

Many Christians – probably most – have their own copies of the Bible for personal rather than corporate use. It is possible to obtain study notes from a variety of sources, enabling the individual reader to work through the Bible in an informed way. Yet it remains true that the most productive way of using the Bible is not in isolation from other Christians, but in company with them. The sharing of ideas and the pooling of insights often yield the best fruit. Churches are now beginning to recognise the value of providing guide-books to the Bible as a part of their Christian education programmes for adults as well as children, though there is still a long way to go in this respect. These guide-books are not restricted to the type commonly referred to as 'spiritually uplifting': they include scholarly accounts of how the Bible came to be written, what has happened to it down the centuries, and how it is currently being understood in the light of modern thinking.

DISCUSSION POINTS

1. Is it really true that the Bible guides the Christian Church in its life and work? Is this not more of a pious hope than an actual reality?

2. How can the Church prevent its members from misinterpreting the Bible?

3. If the Bible is meaningful only in the context of the Church, is it right to study it in secular schools?

4. Can Christians now dispense with the Old Testament, and if not, why not?

5. Must Christians take the Bible literally? If they can pick and choose from its contents, what is the principle of selection?

6. Should Christian sermons always be based on the Bible? Is there a case for preaching on topical issues, without a Biblical text?

7. Is the practice of distributing free copies of the Bible, without comment, a helpful or a dangerous one?

8. What kinds of literature ought to go into a Church library?

9. If modern scholarship has proved that the Bible is the work of human beings, in what sense can Christians still regard it as the Word of God?

15 | Christian Ministry and Priesthood

There are priests in many of the world's religions, and their usual functions are associated with the rituals of sacrifice. In ancient Israel, a priest's role involved the offering of sacrifices in the manner prescribed in the Law, and in the very earliest times this task was commonly performed by the head of the family, because at first there was no official priesthood in existence. Gradually religious practices became more organised, and particular individuals or groups were entrusted with looking after the shrines where sacrifices took place. It is for this reason that priests were always to be found in or near to the sanctuaries – sometimes in very large numbers. Then, when the Temple was built during the reign of King Solomon, the cult was centralised in the holy city of Jerusalem and became pre-eminent, though there were certainly sanctuaries in other places which continued to be used for the offering of sacrifices. These were generally frowned upon by the writers of the Old Testament, who held to the view that there ought to be only one true place of worship.

In those ancient times, the responsibilities of a priest were not what we would now describe as a vocation; priesthood was simply a job. The only occasions where someone was said to be 'called' by God to undertake a particular kind of work were in connection with the monarchy or the prophetic ministry. Priesthood was not a 'calling', and indeed it actually became an inherited responsibility, almost like a skill passed on from father to son, and no special qualities seem to have been required apart from a knowledge of the sacrificial system and its proper routines. After the destruction of the Jewish Temple in AD 70, followed by the dispersion of the Jews, there was no centralised religious observance, and the priesthood was found to be unnecessary apart from the performance of a few ceremonial rituals. Today, Jewish congregations are led by Rabbis (teachers), and not by priests.

Christian priesthood

In the Christian tradition it was accepted from an early date that Christ had offered himself as a sacrifice on the cross, and in that sense he was thought of as the human personification of the sacrificial lamb offered to God on the Temple altar. But it was also claimed that he had taken on the role of the great High Priest, too. He was both the priest and the victim. This is brought out most clearly in the (anonymous) letter to the Hebrews: look at the following passage:

Hebrews 4:14–16

● *Here the writer openly describes Jesus as High Priest, whose work is all the more effective because he shared the nature of those on whose behalf his sacrifice was offered.*

Yet it took some time before the Christian Church came to regard priesthood as a major element in the wider work of Christian ministry. Scholars have noted that it was not until the end of the 2nd century AD that a true Christian priesthood came into being, and even then it was mainly restricted to bishops. Local church leaders were known as presbyters (from which our word 'priest' is actually derived), and they did not at first have any recognisable priestly functions of their own apart from those which they performed as agents of their Bishop.

Gradually, however, local ministers (presbyters) began to undertake such duties as consecrating and administering the Eucharist without the direct involvement of the Bishop, and this prepared the way for a full development of the familiar idea of priesthood as it is today. Nowadays it is normal for local priests to officiate in rites and ceremonies which were formerly the prerogative of Bishops, and they are commonly authorised to do this at their ordination. Priests are in this respect distinguished from deacons, whose authority 'at the altar' is somewhat less.

The views of the Reformers

By the time of the Reformation (from the 15th century) it had become customary to regard the work of a priest as being almost exclusively concerned with the administration of the Sacraments, and especially that of the Mass. Pastoral work was often carried out by the lesser orders and by the laity. It was this which caused the Reformers to question the whole institution of the priesthood as they perceived it to be at that time, and with that questioning there came a widespread rejection of the priestly office. Those who wanted change judged that the priests had lost their awareness of being ministers or servants of Christ and his people, and instead had adopted a hierarchical role which did not seem to match the principles laid down in the New Testament.

Because of this, some of the Reformation churches abandoned not only the priesthood, but also the sacrificial kind of worship which required an altar to be set up in church buildings – so the altar disappeared along with the priesthood, and in its place there stood a Communion Table. The thinking behind this was expressed in a well-known Free Church hymn written by John Harris in the middle of the nineteenth century:

> 'Light up this house with glory, Lord,
> Enter and claim Thine own;
> Receive the homage of our souls,
> Erect Thy temple-throne
>
> We rear no altar – Thou has died,
> We deck no priestly shrine;
> What need have we of creature-aid?
> The power to save is Thine.'

Alongside these ideas there grew up a recognition that, in a sense, all Christians have a 'priestly' role to fill in that they

77

are commissioned to mediate the love of Christ to the world. The concept of a priest as a mediator or 'go-between' has always been present, but now it came into its own as a way of describing the work that all Christians, ordained or lay, are called upon to do. The phrase 'the priesthood of all believers' is still commonly heard, especially in Free Church circles where it is used to affirm the responsibility of every Church member.

Women and the priesthood

One of the consequences of this distinction between priesthood and ministry is that in those churches which have no priests at all (i.e. the Free Churches) there has been a fairly long-standing acceptance of the principle that women can fulfil a ministerial role. There are women ministers in several of these denominations, and they have come to be fully accepted as of equal status to men. But in the churches which have retained the priesthood, the question of the place of women has been much more difficult. The Roman Catholic Church has set its face firmly against the idea of women in the priesthood, and the Church of England is currently passing through a period of considerable difficulty after its recent decision to ordain women. The arguments are not always clear to see, but they involve the claim that a true priest – as distinct from a minister – is someone who is chosen by God, and according to tradition God has always chosen men. It still remains to be seen how this difference of opinion will affect the rank and file of Anglicans, but what it has done is to highlight the distinction between a priest as a 'sacerdotal' figure (i.e. mediating between God and humankind) and a minister (who is essentially a 'servant'). This distinction has largely been overlooked in contemporary Church life.

In the meantime, the concept of 'ministry' itself is developing, both inside and outside the churches which have a conventional priesthood. The distinction between paid and unpaid ministers is disappearing, and questions are beginning to be asked about the nature of ordination itself, and what precisely it is supposed to impart. Ministry is being seen as extending beyond the boundaries of ecclesiastical institutions, and it seems likely that there will be quite far-reaching changes of outlook in the future.

DISCUSSION POINTS

1. What do you understand by the phrase 'the priesthood of all believers'?

2. If the Free Churches have managed without priests since the seventeenth century, does this suggest that priesthood is not essential in the Church?

3. Must the priesthood always be male? What does gender have to do with it?

4. Is priesthood a vocation? Do priests have to be perfect in order to carry out their duties properly? Must they be celibate?

5. If Christ is 'the great High Priest', where does this leave the human priesthood in relation to him?

6. What do you understand to be conferred upon a priest at ordination?

| 16 | **Tradition in the Church** |

Tradition as revelation

The right place to begin a consideration of 'tradition' is to clarify its meaning. It is a word which has caused a great deal of controversy down the centuries, and it has to be admitted that much of the trouble has been due to misunderstandings about what the term signifies. In popular parlance it generally means 'something which has been handed down from earlier times', but this is not what the word means in the New Testament documents, nor is it what the first Christian leaders meant when they used the term. These early writers regarded 'tradition' as something with which they had been entrusted; it was not a collection of revered customs, but a sacred treasure given to them by God through the process of revelation. Its authority did not derive from its antiquity, but from its source. It is true that an ancient tradition was all the more respected because it had stood the test of time, but this was not the reason for its importance. It mattered, not because it was old, but because it was believed to have come from God. St Paul made a clear distinction between those customs which had been invented by human beings and the truth which came from God. Look at the following passage:

Colossians 2:6–8

● *In this passage Paul warns his people against falling prey to 'traditions of man-made teaching', which he evidently considers to be valueless, and advises them instead to become rooted in Jesus, who was 'delivered' to them as Christ and Lord. The idea of 'delivery' is that of the handing-over of something from God – in this context, the true tradition.*

Tradition as accumulated wisdom

Yet the word has also acquired other meanings. In particular, it frequently refers to the accumulated wisdom of the past, which has been preserved for Christian posterity. The pronouncements of Christian leaders and scholars are often regarded as contributing to this constantly-developing store of truth, as also is the witness of those who became martyrs for the sake of Christ and his Church. This kind of tradition could be distinguished from the one described above by its generality. It is a sort of consensus of perceived truth, shared out and passed down as a part of the Church's treasures. In the Roman Catholic Church, and to a somewhat lesser extent in the Church of England, this understanding of tradition has been given considerable importance; it has come to be recognised as a further storehouse of revealed truth, which the Church has received from God.

Tradition as custom

Again, there is a third sense in which the word is sometimes used. It can refer to particular customs or beliefs which have survived for a long time, mainly because no-one has seriously questioned their validity. There are many examples of such 'traditions' in the life of the various churches: habits are formed, founded not upon understanding or critical evaluation, but purely on the basis that these things have always been done. Conversely churches are often reluctant to experiment with unfamiliar ideas for no other reason that they are new and have no traditional precedent – a fact which led to the following parody of a well-known hymn:

> 'Like a mighty tortoise
> Moves the Church of God:
> Brothers, we are treading
> Where we've always trod . . .'

Just as there can be a supposed 'tradition' of doing things in a particular way, so also there can be a 'tradition' of not doing things because they have never been done like that before.

81

The Gospel tradition

Christians have always thought of the Gospel as a 'tradition', and this is a perfectly proper interpretation of it. From the very beginning it was seen to be something revealed by God. It is a message to be delivered. However, sometimes that interpretation has led to the belief that the message, or the 'good news', must always be delivered in the same manner, because the form of it is identified with its contents. Here we see an example of the way in which one use of the word 'tradition' (i.e. the Gospel) is confused with another (the conventional manner of its proclamation). The concept of revelation is mixed up with that of custom, and the outcome is that the central message of Christianity is petrified in its original form.

The idea that a tradition (i.e. a revelation) from God ought to be preserved is roundly condemned in the New Testament. Look at the following passage:

Matthew 25:15–30

● *In this passage Jesus condemns the servant who, in his anxiety to preserve the treasure with which he has been entrusted, buries it in the ground. It was certainly safe there – but it was also utterly unproductive.*

The dangers of traditionalism

The most obvious peril of traditionalism is that, if understood as 'custom', it encourages people to live in the past, and makes them reluctant to change. There is a curious contradiction here. It is common for Protestant churches to point the finger of criticism at the Roman Catholic Church and to accuse it of being held back by its own history – yet Catholicism has always tried to use the past in an evaluative way, measuring the present and the future in the light of standards and norms developed over the centuries. This produces a genuinely critical attitude towards tradition – which sometimes the

Protestant churches do not have. Instead, they can all too easily become dismissive of tradition, as if it were always a hindrance, thereby losing their sense of continuity with their own origins.

Traditionalism, if not treated with care, can lead to excessive formalism, when the things that have always been done become venerated in a superstitious way. Attempts to change patterns of worship, for example, have frequently been met with opposition from those who say that new approaches are unacceptable because they are unfamiliar. Again, it can turn into a kind of legalism, when habit effectively becomes law. Here, the mistake is in thinking that if something has always been done in a particular way, then that is how it must be done, and to do anything else is counted as 'wrong'. A further danger is that it can actually hold the Christian Church back from making any progress at all, resulting in a Church which is so out of touch with the present that it ceases to have anything meaningful to say about it, and even when it does speak, it uses an archaic language which contemporary society cannot understand.

DISCUSSION POINTS

1. How should we measure the value of a tradition? Are there any tests which can be applied?
2. Can we distinguish between what the Gospel says and the manner of its proclamation?
3. Is what is old necessarily out of date, and is what is modern necessarily good?
4. Can you identify any instances where the Church has clung to traditions which it ought to have relinquished?
5. Can we take the past with us into the future?
6. How can we prevent habits and customs from holding the Church back?
7. Are young people less 'traditionalist' than the older generation?

8. **Does the preservation of traditions have a role to play in making people feel secure? Should security be something which a Christian seeks?**

17	**Christian Marriage**

The idea of marriage has existed since the very earliest times. It has usually been understood as a partnership of a man and a woman, living together with the full approval of the other members of the community or society. In the wedding ceremony the couple have made promises expressing their commitment to one another. Although the actual ceremonies have been very different, all of them demonstrate the fundamental idea that marriage is a very serious undertaking, involving not only the two partners but also their wider family and especially the children who may eventually be born to them.

In Britain, as in the western world generally, there has grown up a distinction between the religious and the legal sides of marriage. This is not universally the case; in some eastern countries a marriage is looked upon solely as a religious matter, and a priest has to be present at the wedding ceremony to give a blessing. Without this, the marriage is not considered to be valid. Indeed, it is actually the priest who does the marrying, whereas in western society it is the couple who volunteer themselves to one another.

The Christian view of marriage

The roots of Christian marriage are to be found in the Old Testament idea of the 'covenant'. It was believed that God had set up a special relationship between himself and his people, which bound them together in a permanent bond of love. This was not a contract. Contracts are legal documents or agreements made by equal partners. The Biblical understanding of God's covenant was that the two parties (God and humanity) are not equal, and that God makes the terms of the arrangement. God is the originator of the covenant. He holds it in place, and it cannot be broken by human wilfulness alone, though it can be rendered ineffective. It can be terminated only by God. This idea is reflected in the passage quoted at all Christian wedding ceremonies: 'What God has joined together, let not humans separate'. From this theological starting-point there developed the view that marriage is a reflection of that sacred relationship. There are several places in the Bible where the breaking of the divine covenant is likened to committing adultery.

The Old Testament also suggests that the marriage-bond is a fulfilment of true human nature, in that male and female need each other. The book of Genesis affirms that 'it is not good that man shall be alone', and that a partner is necessary to make him complete. By coming together in marriage, and especially in the physical act of sexual intercourse, male and female become one. The view has been called into question in recent years by some who argue that this is offensive to all those people who have never taken a partner. Jewish customs which derived from this religious view of marriage form the background to the Christian attitude. Historically, the initial step towards marriage was the betrothal or engagement, which involved the payment of a dowry to the father of the bride. This period of engagement was treated very seriously indeed, and the future bride was expected to conduct herself in a manner which reflected the fact that she was already promised to her future husband. Then, after a suitable period of time, the actual wedding took place, followed by a feast – the lavishness of which depended upon how wealthy the family were. The marriage was considered to be a lifelong commitment, and the prospect of divorce was almost too awful to contemplate. Only in the most extreme circumstances could it be allowed.

In the time of Jesus, attitudes to marriage had begun to change. Greek influences were strong, and the Greek culture permitted easy divorce. Jewish ideas had also changed: the understanding of the complementariness of the two sexes had to some extent given way to a system in which women were thought of as the property of their husbands, with very few legal rights. Marriage was frequently thought of as a duty rather than as a lifelong commitment or an act of fulfilment. Divorce was also becoming more common. A simple writ or certificate, handed to the wife by the husband in the presence of two witnesses, was sufficient to end a marriage. It may have been for this reason that Jesus spoke out on the subject, calling people back to the earlier principles. Look at the following passage:

Matthew 19:1–9

● *St Matthew here records the teaching of Jesus about*
  marriage and divorce, stressing the ideals of the book of
  Genesis, and saying that the changes had taken place
  because people had become insensitive or blind to the first
  principles.

Changing attitudes to marriage

In the sixteenth century divorce was virtually unknown in Britain, apart from a few cases where people of high social rank were able to obtain special dispensations. A change took place, however, when in the nineteenth century the government made it possible for people to enter into a legal valid marriage in a registry office as distinct from a place of worship, and this new arrangement included the freedom of registrars to re-marry divorced persons – something which the Roman Catholic and Anglican Churches would not countenance. The new laws also forbade the Church from taking any action against its own priests who decided to officiate at such re-marriages, though this began to happen more and more frequently.

Gradually the picture changed. Many clergy, especially in the Free Churches but also in the Church of England, began to take the view that the Christian doctrine of forgiveness took precedence over the more legalistic view of marriage as indissoluble, and felt that it was right in some circumstances to give divorced people an opportunity for a fresh start – especially if they were the 'innocent parties'.

In more recent times there have been changes of a different kind. Now the burning question is not that of whether divorce ought to be permitted by the Christian Church, but whether marriage itself is of any significance. A growing number of people are setting up home together, having children, and establishing partnerships without the 'formalities' of any kind of wedding, whether it be in a Church or in a registry office. Whereas a few generations ago it was socially unacceptable for people to be divorced, or for children to be born outside marriage, today's society appears to be much more tolerant, regarding divorce and single-parent families as normal. The question being asked is whether the Christian view of marriage has any meaning or relevance in contemporary society, especially when it is plain that marriages begun in a church are just as prone to breakdown as those which take place in registry offices. Marriage certificates are often referred to as 'bits of paper', and the claim is made that what holds people together is not the ceremony which is supposed to bind them, but the love which they have for one another. The concept of trial marriages – commonly found in some other cultures – has found its way into western society.

In addition, questions are being asked about the propriety of partnerships between people of the same sex. There are numerous instances of Christian ministers and clergy being asked to conduct 'marriage ceremonies' for homosexual couples, and to bless their 'union' in the same way as for conventional couples. Arguments about the nature of love itself, and the place of sexual activity within or without the marriage bond, are currently causing a great deal of debate. This is happening alongside the continuance of older practices such as celibacy in the Roman Catholic priesthood, and the current picture is one of great confusion.

DISCUSSION POINTS

1. What do you understand by the Biblical claim that, in marriage, two people become one?

2. What do you consider to be the essential difference between a marriage ceremony performed in a church and one performed in a registry office?

3. What ought to be the Christian position with regard to the matter of divorce? Is the idea of marriage until death still meaningful? What is a Christian view of the 'irretrievable breakdown' of a marriage? What about loveless marriages or marriages of convenience?

4. Is the idea of 'trial marriage' acceptable to a Christian?

5. Can Christians accept that homosexual partnerships are true marriages?

6. If one kind of church refuses to conduct the marriage of divorcees, while another kind of church is willing to do it, what kind of message is signalled to the non-Christian?

7. Is it a Christian view that people are somehow incomplete if they are unmarried?

8. Is marriage mainly intended for the procreation of children in a secure family environment?

9. Can a Christian approve of the idea of arranged marriages, such as those found in Asian countries?

10. Would it offend Christian principles if it could be shown that Jesus was married, as some have seriously suggested?

18 | Christianity and Politics

It is not at all uncommon to hear the Christian Church accused of 'dabbling in politics', and there have been numerous instances in recent times of high-ranking politicians warning Church leaders to restrict themselves to spiritual affairs, and not to interfere in political issues. However, to make such a separation is to misunderstand the nature of the Christian Gospel. Since politics is all about the management of societies, and their relations with each other, it is quite impossible for Christians to stand back and avoid becoming involved. There may be a case for saying that party politics (i.e. alignment with a particular political group) is out of place in a Christian pulpit, but that is very different from saying that Christians ought to have no interest in the way in which governments exercise their authority. To opt out of that area of life would be to opt out of issues of human relations and human rights. It would be to create the impression that the religious life belongs to some other world than this one. The Christian religion, with its teaching about the incarnation, stresses the principle of God at work in human affairs, and cannot withdraw into an abstract kind of spirituality from which human relationship are excluded.

Politics in the Old Testament

Even a superficial study of the Old Testament, and especially of the prophetic writings, quickly reveals the extent to which religion and politics were intertwined. We find Isaiah of Jerusalem making highly political statements about the Egyptians (see Isaiah 19:1ff), and Jeremiah warning his own people of impending invasion, which he regarded as God's divine judgement (see Jeremiah 5:15ff). In the eighth century BC the prophet Amos was highly critical of the contemporary state of affairs in Israel, condemning the corruption that existed in commerce and the law courts (see Amos 5:7–15). In the period of the monarchy it was normal for kings and military leaders to consult the prophets before embarking upon political action, highlighting the fact that no sharp distinction was made between religion and government.

Politics in the New Testament

One of the charges levelled against Jesus by his opponents was that he was engaged in political upheaval, claiming to be a king and thereby posing a threat to Roman authority. Despite the fact that, according to the author of the Fourth Gospel, Jesus refused to make political claims for himself (see John 18:33–40), it is plain that his teachings did have political implications. This became very obvious when St Paul began to spread the Christian faith in the Gentile world: he was in political trouble almost as soon as he started his work, being placed under arrest several times along with other leading Christians. Look at the following passage:

Acts 17:5–9

● *Paul and Silas are in trouble not only with the Jewish authorities but also with the Roman magistrates, and suspected of being political dissidents who are breaking the law and undermining the authority of the Emperor.*

The political implications of the Christian Gospel

Any religion which asserts (as Christianity does) that all people are equal under God, and have equal rights under the law, is bound to find itself caught up in issues where those human rights are at risk. Christians have never felt that their role is to do no more than shout advice from the touchlines of society; instead they have become deeply involved both in caring for those who are victims of social and political wrongdoing, and also in working to prevent political corruption at all levels. The notion that all life is sacred inevitably leads to demands that anything which demeans humanity shall be opposed, no matter from what source the threat might come.

In more recent times the theology of redemption – so deeply embedded in Christian thought – has found expression in what has come to be known as liberation theology. This has focussed its attention upon the Gospel as being essentially 'good news for the poor'. It came to the surface, though not under that name, in Christian pressures for the abolition of the slave trade, pioneered by William Wilberforce. In 1787 he wrote these words in his diary:

'God Almighty has set before me two great objects, the suppression of the slave trade and the reformation of manners . . .'

Later on, in a speech made to Parliament, he said:

'Already we have gained one victory; we have obtained, for these poor creatures, the recognition of their human nature, which, for a while, was most shamefully denied . . . Never, never will we desist till we have wiped away this scandal from the Christian name . . .'.

Now, liberation theology has emerged again in the form of Christian condemnation of political regimes which practice the suppression of human rights, and one can see much of this in the situation in South Africa, though it is by no means limited to that country.

Christianity and the State

It is sometimes considered to be strange that in Britain, where the Christian religion is built into the actual establishment of the constitution, there should still be those who complain that it ought to be separated from it. Since the monarch is both Head of State and titular Head of the Church of England, such a separation could come about only by changing the constitution itself. Yet the reasoning behind the 'disestablishment' lobby is that if the Church were free from state involvement (as are the Free Churches already), it would be easier for Christians to speak out on political issues. Those who want to retain the Church-State partnership, on the other hand, claim that the Church can be more influential from the inside than from the outside. It is already the case that bishops have a place in the House of Lords, and are thus able to influence government policies.

For the most part, the political activism of Christians has taken the form of voting for a parliamentary candidate whose policies most closely approximate to the Christian ideal. Sometimes this has resulted in the support of one particular party, and sometimes another has presented itself as more acceptable. In some countries there are actually political parties which have taken their stand on Christian principles and included the word 'Christian' in their name. However, in view of the fact that there are many issues on which Christians are themselves not in accord, it cannot be said that one political stance rather than another is always an obvious choice for winning the Christian vote.

DISCUSSION POINTS

1. Could there ever be such a thing as a truly Christian political party? If so, what would its manifesto look like? Would it ever be elected into government?

2. Do the Jehovah's Witnesses have a point when they insist that all forms of human government must be subservient to the rule of God? Does this mean that a Christian should never vote for any of them?

3. How deeply can a Christian become involved in political activity without becoming compromised?

4. Should the Christian Church be entirely distinct from the State?

5. Can political principles be the same as religious principles?

6. If a parliamentary candidate seeking election were to

appear before a Christian audience, what questions might that audience put to him or her?

7. **Should politicians be asked not to meddle in religion?**

<table>
<tr><td>**19**</td><td>**Christian Education**</td></tr>
</table>

This Topic differs from the others in that it is in the form of a deliberately-provocative challenge to the Christian churches to treat education seriously. It will be seen that it is in the nature of a justification for the writing of these Study Notes: so there is a sense in which it is perhaps in the wrong place, because a group which is using these notes is already well on the way towards solving the problems which are highlighted here.

A concern for education has always been a central feature of the Christian religion. According to the New Testament, Jesus himself spent a great deal of his time engaged in teaching, and his closest followers were regarded as apprentices or learners. They sat at his feet to listen to his instruction, as he expounded his ideas and prepared them for their own work as advocates of the Gospel. Again, the letters of St Paul reveal the extent to which he acted as a teacher to his congregations, as well as a pastor. This concern for learning was deeply embedded in the Jewish religion, and it is no accident that synagogues were always regarded as places of study as well as places of worship.

The pioneering work of the Churches in education

Historically, the great establishments of learning were commonly religious institutions, and it was the pioneering work of the Christian churches which led to the setting-up of schools in Britain. Prior to 1870 there was no state system of education in existence: virtually all schools were in the hands of the churches, apart from a few which had been founded by charitable bodies of other kinds. Even when the state became involved, it was openly said that the intention was not to replace the church schools but to fill in the gaps in the provision which they had made. Today, the dual system of a partnership between state and church schools still continues, and Religious Education is a legally-required area of the curriculum, even in those schools which are in the hands of the secular authorities. School Worship is also still required by law. However, there is now a recognition that the Christian religion is not the only faith which is to be found in Britain, and other religions have a place.

The Sunday School Movement, usually associated with the work of Robert Raikes in the eighteenth century, began as an attempt to instruct children in the basics of reading and in the fundamentals of the Christian religion. At first it was a somewhat fragmented system, but the founding of the Sunday School Union in 1803 helped to give it a broader structure and provided books and other materials. Then, as general education improved, the Sunday Schools focussed their work upon Christian education, and those who taught within them were able to receive a more adequate training through the setting-up of a college in Birmingham. Today, many Sunday Schools have been given the name of Junior Church (or 'Children's Church'), illustrating a growing awareness that the children are not merely being prepared for future membership, but are regarded as already within the church family here and now.

Adult Education in the Churches

The concentration of the churches upon the work of instructing their own children has led to a widespread neglect of adult education. References to Christian Education in most churches are immediately understood to mean the work going on among the younger generation, and it is sometimes difficult to find much evidence of any continuing programme of learning in which the adult members are involved. Obviously there will be exceptions to this, but on the whole there is a common assumption made that learning comes to an end on leaving school or college. The hope is that the adult congregation will receive their instruction from the pulpit during the Sunday services of worship, but this hope is rarely fulfilled because it is quite impracticable. Some of the churches try to meet the need by organising study groups, but not all are successful, and in any case most of the them are restricted to a 'devotional' exploration of the text of the Bible, leaving enormous areas of Christian thought and practice completely untouched.

As a direct outcome of this situation there has grown up a frightening gulf between the leaders of Christian thought and the 'average church member'. The fruits of religious scholarship, although there for the picking, have not been fully harvested. Many church members have no idea of what has been going on in the development of Christian understanding, and are utterly unskilled in dealing with important religious issues. Then, when new ideas are brought into the foregound, there is often a widespread panic – well illustrated by the reaction to certain publications of allegedly heretical bishops over the past generation. The point has been reached where, for some Christians, it is considered wicked even to contemplate the possibility that some parts of the Bible could be in error, or that some revered Christian customs might be changed.

The concept of a church as a place of study as well as a place of worship has largely been lost. Few churches have put the continuing education of their adult members very high on their list of priorities, and although it is not at all unusual to find a bookstall located somewhere on the premises, the possibility of setting up a church library has rarely been explored. Even the bookstall is often stocked with simplistic material of a 'spiritually uplifting' kind, rather than with substantial books which can open up the world of religious scholarship to the enquiring church member.

Understanding as a preliminary to evangelism

It almost goes without saying that, if the members of the Christian Church (of any denomination) are to carry out their responsibility of spreading their faith, they must be properly equipped to do it. Good will is not enough. The average non-churchgoer is full of awkward questions about what the Christian religion teaches, why it does things in certain ways, how it deals with such difficulties as belief in God or the problem of suffering, and what difference it makes to be a Christian anyway. These questions need to be faced by the Church itself before it attempts to deal with them in the context of debate with the 'outside world'. Pious answers about trusting in God or 'having faith' simply will not meet the needs of the modern questioner, who often genuinely wants to know what the Christian religion has to offer. In short, the present age is one in which – perhaps more than at any other time – the Church must teach itself before it tries to teach others.

DISCUSSION POINTS

1. Should the Christian pulpit be used for Christian teaching rather than for preaching?

2. Education forms a very large part of the nation's budget. Ought this to be true in the churches? Do churches spend enough time and money on teaching their own people?

3. How can the yawning gap between the present position of Christian leaders and the 'average Christian' be bridged? Where do we start? Is it the leaders themselves who have lost touch with their people?

4. Is there anything wrong with asking questions about matters of Christian life and belief? Are such questions indicative of a lack of faith? Is there such a thing as honest doubt? Or are those who refuse to ask questions the ones whose faith is insecure?

5. Can Christian Education be confined to studying the Bible? Or is there more to it than that?

6. Is Confirmation/Church Membership the beginning or the end of the Christian quest? Is it where learning starts, or where it finishes?

7. If state schools can no longer use Religious Education lessons for the purpose of recruiting children into the churches, where does this leave the churches?

8. Should ministers/clergy be better trained to deal with the work of Christian Education?

9. What do you understand by the phrase 'growing in the faith'?

10. What is the difference between preaching and teaching?

20 Diversity and Division in the Church

It is not at all difficult to see that the Christian Church is divided. This is not the place to go into the question of when and how these divisions came into being, but the vast proliferation of churches and denominations bears witness to the seriousness of the situation. Even the smallest town or village has its distinct congregations, sometimes co-existing happily and sometimes not. The nature of the divisions is itself very confused, with churches standing apart from one another for a whole range of different reasons.

Christian diversity

It could be argued that this state of affairs is not necessarily a bad thing. Just as shoppers like to pick and choose between different stores in order to find a bargain, so also (it is said) Christians like to have some choice in the kind of church to which they will give their allegiance. Patterns of worship vary, so that an individual's personal tastes can be accommodated. This kind of argument is really another way of saying that there is no serious division in the Church at all – there is just variety, and that is to be commended because it enables different needs to be met. Sometimes this claim is extended by adding that although the churches and denominations are all different from one another, nevertheless there is a sort of spiritual unity which binds them all together.

It is certainly the case that worship can take many forms. It is also true that there has to be room for variety in the expression of Christian truth. Diversity is essential if the Church is not to be condemned to a dull sameness at all times and in places. However, there is a point at which diversity becomes division, and the enjoyment of variety of worship leads to the destruction of a common life. When people can no longer bring themselves to worship together with others because the forms of that worship make it impossible, something has clearly gone wrong.

Christian disunity

To the casual observer it might seem as if the only difference between one kind of church and another is in the nature of the services of worship. The truth, however, is that the divisions go much deeper than that. Many of them have to do with the question of how the church is run – who is its leader, where its policy decisions are made, and how it is structured. There are serious differences of view concerning the nature and authority of the ministry, and even in the whole concept of what a church really is. Some of the earlier Topics in this series have brought these differences to the surface, especially those which deal with the Sacraments and with the question 'What is a Church?'. Furthermore, the task of spreading the Gospel has been seriously hampered by the fact that it is impossible to preach about Christ bringing people together in love when his own churches do not work or think in harmony with one another.

The Ecumenical Movement

During this century there have been great advances made in the pursuit of Christian unity. The World Council of Churches has provided a platform for the sharing of ideas and experiences, and there has grown up a much greater understanding of one another's positions. It is true, however, that not a great deal has been achieved in terms of actual churches coming together: the only significant instance of such a union in Britain was the formation of the United Reformed Church in 1972, when English Presbyterians and Congregationalists agreed to unite under a new name and with a new constitution. But even that was not a complete success, and there are numerous continuing Congregational churches which still stand apart from it. Some other smaller churches have since joined, but the initial impetus has slowed. Other attempts to unite different churches (such as the Anglican/Methodist conversations) have generally failed, and serious divisions still remain. Meanwhile, the Roman Catholic Church holds firmly to its view that unity will come about only when all the differing churches come together within its fold, accepting the authority of the Pope.

Theological divisions

The churches are sometimes divided over such matters as the proper interpretation of the Bible, or the necessity of a conversion experience as a sign of being a true Christian. Divisions of this nature are not strictly denominational, though sometimes they do have implications of that kind. Within the ranks of the Church of England there has been a serious problem sparked off by the decision to ordain women into the priesthood, and this seems likely to result in further splits in the ranks, with some Anglicans moving towards the Roman Catholic Church, and others trying to set up some kind of alternative structure within (or on the brink of) the Church of England.

Unity and uniformity

The most common obstacle in the quest for Christian unity is the fear that all churches will be compelled to be the same. The word 'uniformity' is much used in this context. Christians worry that they will lose their cherished variety and their freedom to experiment or to be creative. Despite the efforts made to reassure them that unity and uniformity are two different things, this fear persists, and experience has shown that, even with those reassurances, some measure of uniformity, or conformity to general patterns, is a price that has to be paid. Like the word 'uniformity', the term 'freedom' is commonly on the agenda of unity discussions, and the question then is the extent to which the exercise of freedom of religion can actually result in the loss of any sense of direction. Freedom is not licence. Even the so-called 'Free Churches' have generally acknowledged that there are limits to what they can do if they are to retain a genuine fellowship with other Christians. They are still 'under orders', but now those orders derive from the nature of the Gospel and not from the directives issued by an ecclesiastical hierarchy.

Christians and other religions

One of the reasons why there seems to have been a slowing-down in the pursuit of Christian unity is that, more and more, the churches are having to come to terms with the nature of their relation to people of other religions altogether. In the face of this situation, with Britain becoming a multi-faith society, the search for unity between the churches begins to look like a very parochial matter indeed, and one which is far less urgent.

DISCUSSION POINTS

1. At what point does diversity end and division begin?

2. Are the divisions between the churches really very serious? Is this something that Christians must accept as a reflection of the many ways in which God is perceived?

3. Is there any truth in the suggestion that the quest for Christian unity owes more to the declining number of church-goers than to any theology of unity?

4. What do you understand by the words 'spiritual unity' as a description of what it is that holds the churches together? Does the idea express something real, or is it just a pretext for avoiding the fact of division?

5. Why is it that the Church finds it so easy to split, and so hard to unite?

6. Where must the quest for unity begin – at the 'top' or at the 'grass roots'?

7. Are the divisions within the Church ever reflected in the life of particular congregations? If they are, how are they dealt with there?

8. To what extent does unity require uniformity? If all the churches did everything in exactly the same ways, would unity have been achieved?

9. If the churches must now seek to establish relations with other religious faiths, does that mean that the quest for Christian unity can be abandoned?

10. What did Jesus mean when he prayed 'that all might be one'?

<table>
<tr><td>

21

</td><td>

Christianity and Other Religions

</td></tr>
</table>

What attitude should a Christian adopt towards the other religions of the world? If we were to interpret this question as meaning 'how should a Christian treat people from other religious traditions?', then the answer would be straightforward: the proper attitude must be the same as it is towards everyone else. The principle of Christian love demands that no distinction be made between Christian and non-Christian, rich and poor, or black and white, and the parable of the Good Samaritan (Luke 10:25–37) brings this home very forcibly. However, this is not what the question means. We are asked to consider what attitude a Christian ought to take up towards the actual religions themselves, rather than towards those who subscribe to them. How does Christianity respond to (for example) Islam, or Hinduism, or Buddhism, or Sikhism, or even its own parent-religion of Judaism? Does it reject them as being false? Does it welcome them as 'doing the same job' but in a different way? Does it see them as partners in the quest for the good life, or as enemies to be overcome? In short, are they a threat, or are they allies in the fight against irreligion?

Is there a Biblical view?

The early parts of the Old Testament make it clear that the Hebrew people regarded themselves as God's chosen people, and that their God was the only God who mattered. Other deities were to be opposed, and the faithful Israelites were instructed to have no gods other than YAHWEH (which is the more correct form of the old word JEHOVAH). Look at the following passage:

Exodus 20:1–6

● *This familiar passage from the Ten Commandments*

105

*establishes the principle that for the Chosen People (the
Hebrews) there can be no other deity. However, the
injunction clearly presupposes that other deities do exist,
otherwise there would be no point in issuing a warning
against following them. It is only later that the prophets
began to teach that other gods did not even exist.*

When, after their release from slavery in Egypt, they found
their way into Canaan, one of the most urgent tasks facing the
Hebrews was to establish their own religion and to work out
their policy towards the religions of the Canaanite tribes –
which were, of course, not all the same. But this evidently was
not easy, and according to one of the earliest accounts the
Hebrew people quickly found themselves adapting to other
religious customs, rather than fighting them off. Look at:

Judges 2:11–15

● *This account was written by someone who was evidently
hostile to the practice of giving up Yahweh-worship in
favour of a different deity.*

But by the eighth century BC there had come about an increasing awareness that Yahweh was the only God, and that other
deities had no real existence. This view became stronger, so
that in the sixth century BC it was being openly and clearly
stated by the unknown prophet who is generally referred to as
Second Isaiah. Look at the following passage:

Isaiah 45:5–7

● *This remarkable passage not only establishes the principle
that there is only one God: it also faces up to what that
belief implies – i.e. that this one God must therefore be
responsible for everything that happens, and is the author
of both prosperity and trouble.*

What is the Christian position?

The Old Testament reflects the conventional Jewish outlook,

and cannot automatically be transferred uncritically to Christianity. Certainly the belief that there is only one God is taken up in Christian thought, but there is a notable softening of the rigid rejection of other faiths. For example, all of the Gospels suggest that Jesus was sympathetic towards the position of Samaritans, whose religion differed in certain important respects from mainstream Judaism. Luke's reference to the Samaritan who thanked Jesus (Luke 17:11–19) shows that the ancient enmity between Jews and Samaritans was not something which Jesus himself accepted. Again, in the Fourth Gospel the same sympathy is evident, so much so that Jesus is actually thought to be a Samaritan himself (see John 8:48).

It is against this background of sensitivity towards people of other faiths that we have to interpret the much-quoted passage in John 14:6, where Jesus is reported as saying that no-one comes to the Father except by (or 'through') him. Taken on its own and out of context this verse appears to dismiss all other religions as false trails, but when it is set over against the much more powerful spirit of understanding, sympathy and toleration demonstrated by Jesus in his dealing with people, it looks much less rigid.

The changing situation

In today's world, religions do not and cannot keep themselves to themselves. With the advent of technology it is easy for ideas to flow around the globe, and for people to move from one culture to another. Religions are no longer territorial: they travel, and are planted in all sorts of places. Those which involve themselves in missionary activity now find that their work is far easier in terms of gaining access to potential converts.

In Britain, the picture has changed radically during the present century. There are now more Muslims in Britain than there are Methodists, and places of worship (Muslim mosques, Sikh

Gurdwaras, Hindu Temples, etc.) are being established in many parts of the country, especially in larger cities. The Christian churches, by contrast, are generally declining both in numbers and in influence. It is now crucially important that these different religions learn to understand one another better, and seek areas of common ground. No longer can Christians rely upon numerical superiority as a means of keeping other religions 'in their place'. Nor can they fall back upon the easy option of claiming that all religions are basically the same under the surface, and that 'we are all going the same way but by different routes', because increasing knowledge of the world's religions clearly shows that this is not the case.

It is also important for Christians to recognise that there are many people in Britain and across the world who subscribe to no religion at all. These cannot be written off as unthinking or apathetic: they are often intelligent and thoughtful people who have concluded that it is perfectly possible to get through life – and to be happy – without turning to any of the religious systems. Christians will have to work out their relation to these, too, and clarify their response to the issues which are raised.

DISCUSSION POINTS

1. Does the Christian principle of loving one's neighbour extend to loving his religion too?

2. To what extent is a religion bound up with a specific culture? Can we change people's religion and leave their cultural practices untouched?

3. Does the principle of freedom of religion mean that Christians should leave other religions alone?

4. If we are to understand other religions, where do we start?

5. Do you approve of opening up Christian churches for inter-faith worship? Is it a positive step towards good relations, or is it a betrayal of Christian principles?

6. Is inter-faith worship possible, if the worshippers all have differing ideas of God?

7. What might Christians be prepared to give up in their own religion, in the interests of finding a common faith?

8. If other religions such as Islam are growing in size and influence, while Christianity is apparently declining, what conclusions should we draw, and what can be done about the situation?

9. Should children in schools be taught about other religions at the expense of Christianity?

10. Is it true that by learning about other religions we can come to see our own in a different light?

22	# The Kingdom of God

The Kingdom of God in the teaching of Jesus

There is one theme which runs right through the Gospels of the New Testament, and which is actually represented as the central feature of the message of Jesus. That theme is the Kingdom of God. Sometimes the phrase 'the Kingdom of Heaven' is used instead, but there is no appreciable difference in the meaning. In the Gospel of Mark the term (in one or other of the two forms) occurs fourteen times. In Matthew's Gospel it is used thirty-seven times, and in Luke's Gospel it appears thirty-two times. Jesus is said to have opened his ministry by preaching on this theme (see Mark 1:14–15), and it is a constant feature of his parables.

Evidently Jesus believed that the Kingdom of God had somehow been inaugurated in himself. He spoke of it as having actually come already. Yet he also spoke of it as something which was still to be finalised, that is, as lying in the future waiting to be turned into a full reality. When he taught his followers to pray, his 'model prayer' included a petition that the Kingdom of God would come on earth, as it already is present in Heaven (see Matthew 6:9–13 and the parallel version in Luke 11:1–4).

Eschatology

This teaching forms part of what scholars refer to by the somewhat daunting name of 'eschatology'. It has to do with teachings about the last days, or the 'end time', when God's plans will be accomplished and his purposes for creation fulfilled. Both Jews and Christians have always held the view that history is going somewhere, and that there is a genuine goal towards which things are moving. We can see this powerful element of forward-looking in the Old Testament, especially in the teachings of the great prophets. It is also inherent in the Jewish expectation of the coming of God's Messiah. The Old Testament actually ends on that kind of note, with a stern warning about a coming day of judgement and the arrival of what Jews called 'the day of the Lord'.

The same notion of looking forward is also present in the New Testament, but there it is transformed because it is associated with the coming of Christ. He has 'set the ball rolling', so the end-time is in that sense thought to be nearer than the somewhat remote expectation of the Old Testament. Christ's life and work mark the beginning of the end. The eschatological ideas begin to collect around the expectation that Christ, after his death and resurrection, will return to bring God's kingdom into being.

What is the nature of the Kingdom of God?

Many different pictures and analogies are offered in the New Testament, and groups may wish to study these in greater depth. Sometimes these images are couched very strongly in Jewish terms, such as the picture painted in the book of Revelation, of the Holy City of Jerusalem coming down from Heaven and being established here on earth (see Revelation 21:1ff). But one thing can be said: the word 'kingdom' does not generally refer to a place or a domain, as it does in the modern sense of the term. Rather, it refers to the actual kingly rule itself, and some scholars have preferred to think of it as God's KINGSHIP or divine authority. Its manifestation is expressed in terms of a universal obedience to God's authority and a total acceptance of his will.

The quest for a perfect world

In modern language Christians might prefer to picture the Kingdom of God as a perfect world, in which everyone is a

Christian. It might be a world in which all wrongs are righted, all suffering is banished, and all people live together in love and charity with their neighbours. In some Christian quarters the convention has been to identify the Christian Church itself as the nucleus of such a world – a sort of Kingdom of God within the kingdoms of humankind. This idea may possibly lie behind the curious passage in Matthew's Gospel (chapter 16:19) where Jesus promises to give to St Peter the keys of the Kingdom: yet the connecting of the Church with the Kingdom has never been a major theme of Christian doctrine, and the teaching cannot be definitely found in early theology, though it did become more general after the time of St Augustine. It is a teaching which has been modified by those who argue that the Church is essentially a means to an end, and not an end in itself. It is commissioned to work for the full inauguration of God's Kingdom, but it is not to be viewed as the Kingdom in embryo because it is as yet far from perfect, and does not truly manifest the characteristics of God's rule.

The Kingdom of God as the Church's goal

By raising the topic of the Kingdom of God, we are really posing the most crucial question of all for the Church of today, and that is to ask 'Where is it all leading?'. Christians are continually confronted with the issue of their aims and objectives. Why is the Church here? What is it for? What is it trying to do? Does it exist for itself, or for others? Questions of this nature constantly have to be asked, and also answered, because it is a feature both of human nature in general and of the church in particular that it is all too easy to lose sight of one's goal. Christian fellowships can quickly fall prey to the habit of existing rather than moving forward, and thus lose sight of their first vision. It is a salutary exercise for churches of all kinds to pause in the midst of their general activities and ask themselves whether what they are doing is genuinely contributing to the advancement of God's Kingdom, or whether they have filled up their diaries with things that lead nowhere in particular. The alleviation of human suffering, the quest for peace on earth, and the hope of a perfect world all have to be translated into achievable objectives rather than left as vague dreams.

DISCUSSION POINTS

1. What is the commission that has been given to the Christian Church? Is it living up to its calling?

2. If the Church really is made up of the people of God, does that give them a special status or a special responsibility?

3. What are the characteristics of the Kingdom of God? Can they ever be realised, or are they just a pious hope?

4. Christianity has been in the world for almost two thousand years: so why has God's Kingdom still not been realised?

5. In what sense can a twentieth-century Christian still believe in the imminent return of Christ?

6. If Christ's work still has to be finished off, was it therefore a failure?

7. Do all church activities contribute towards the establishment of the Kingdom of God? Or are some of them merely social activities for the enjoyment of the church members?

8. Is the Church the only agent of God's Kingdom? Could non-religious bodies be working towards the same end?

LIST OF BIBLE REFERENCES